MW00427399

The Cure for Unjust Anger

SERIES EDITORS
Joel R. Beeke & Jay T. Collier

Interest in the Puritans continues to grow, but many people find the reading of these giants of the faith a bit unnerving. This series seeks to overcome that barrier by presenting Puritan books that are convenient in size and unintimidating in length. Each book is carefully edited with modern readers in mind, smoothing out difficult language of a bygone era while retaining the meaning of the original authors. Books for the series are thoughtfully selected to provide some of the best counsel on important subjects that people continue to wrestle with today.

The Cure for Unjust Anger

John Downame

Edited by
Brian G. Hedges

Reformation Heritage Books
Grand Rapids, Michigan

The Cure for Unjust Anger
© 2020 by Reformation Heritage Books

All rights reserved. No part of this book may be used or reproduced in any manner whatsoever without written permission except in the case of brief quotations embodied in critical articles and reviews. Direct your requests to the publisher at the following addresses:

Reformation Heritage Books
2965 Leonard St. NE
Grand Rapids, MI 49525
616-977-0889
orders@heritagebooks.org
www.heritagebooks.org

Originally published in 1600 as *Spiritual Physick to Cure the Diseases of the Soul, Arising from Superfluitie of Choller, Prescribed out of God's Word*

Printed in the United States of America
20 21 22 23 24 25/10 9 8 7 6 5 4 3 2 1

Library of Congress Cataloging-in-Publication Data

Names: Downame, John, -1652, author. | Hedges, Brian G., editor.
Title: The cure for unjust anger / John Downame ; edited by Brian G. Hedges.
Other titles: Spiritual physick to cure the diseases of the soul, arising from superfluitie
    of choller, prescribed out of God's Word
Description: Grand Rapids, Michigan : Reformation Heritage Books, 2020. |
    Series: Puritan treasures for today | "Originally published in 1600 as Spiritual
    Physick to Cure the Diseases of the Soul, Arising from Superfluitie of Choller,
    Prescribed out of God's Word." | Includes bibliographical references.
Identifiers: LCCN 2020011007 (print) | LCCN 2020011008 (ebook) | ISBN
    9781601787675 (paperback) | ISBN 9781601787682 (epub)
Subjects: LCSH: Anger—Religious aspects—Christianity—Early works to 1800. |
    Christian life—Puritan authors—Early works to 1800.
Classification: LCC BV4627.A5 D685 2020 (print) | LCC BV4627.A5 (ebook) |
    DDC 241/.3—dc23
LC record available at https://lccn.loc.gov/2020011007
LC ebook record available at https://lccn.loc.gov/2020011008

For additional Reformed literature, request a free book list from Reformation Heritage Books at the above regular or e-mail address.

He that is slow to anger is better than the mighty;
and he that ruleth his spirit than he that taketh a city.
—Proverbs 16:32

Table of Contents

Preface

There is a big difference between knowing there is a problem and knowing how to solve it. This is true in every realm of life, not least the medical.

When my oldest son was ten years old, he became very ill. My wife, Holly, and I noticed his lethargy, loss of appetite, and increasingly washed-out, sickly appearance. Holly quickly took him to our pediatrician, who diagnosed him with a mild, passing virus. He would be better in a few days.

But he wasn't. He was getting worse, so Holly took him again. They ran a couple of tests, found nothing wrong, and sent Stephen home. But by Friday of that week, he was just skin and bones. Our usually extroverted, fun-loving ten-year-old was stuck on the couch with no energy and no appetite, his face more pallid by the day. We were very concerned. Holly called the pediatrician again and, refusing to be put off for the weekend, insisted on bringing him in that afternoon. This time I went with her.

Once again, the pediatrician on call could find nothing wrong. Then she decided to do a urinalysis. After a few minutes, she asked if we had a history of diabetes in the family, then left us again for a few minutes. Naturally alarmed, we started reading about symptoms of diabetes on WebMD. Before the doctor returned, we knew that Stephen had DKA—diabetic ketoacidosis.

His life was in danger. His pancreas had stopped producing insulin, the hormone necessary for processing carbohydrates and utilizing sugar in the body. His blood sugar and ketones were dangerously high, his blood was acidic, and his internal organs were not functioning properly. The doctor sent us straight to the hospital— and straight to the pediatric unit. "Don't go home, don't collect two hundred dollars," she said. We weren't even to go through registration and admitting. Stephen was very, very sick and needed immediate attention.

Next was the short, sobering trip to the hospital; then, several hours of waiting for some assurance that our son would be okay; and finally, a clear diagnosis: Stephen had type 1 diabetes. And then we had a crash course in how to manage this disease.

As I write, Stephen is now seventeen, is managing diabetes well, and is back to his extroverted, fun-loving personality in every way. The Lord was merciful and has even used diabetes to help draw Stephen into a deeper dependence on Christ. But our experience reinforced for us a truth that every person must learn: clear diagnosis is essential for proper treatment. The reason Stephen languished with DKA for almost a week was because the doctors and nurses who first saw him misdiagnosed his symptoms. I'm so thankful that Holly's "mom-sense" outweighed their reluctance to see him for that third visit, pushing them to look deeper for the cause of his symptoms.

Clear diagnosis is essential for proper treatment. This is as true in the spiritual life as it is in the physical. For when the maladies of the soul are misdiagnosed, moral mischief and mayhem are sure to follow. Unmortified sin always breeds more sin. Mismanaged soul-care is spiritual malpractice. And that is one reason the Puritans are so valuable today.

The Puritans and Soul-Care

No era in the history of Christ's church has left us with a greater wealth of literature on Christian soul-care than that of the seventeenth-century English Puritans. The Puritans were pastor-theologians extraordinaire. As theologians, they mined the depths of the sacred Scriptures with profound reverence for their divine authority and an earnest desire to elucidate the whole of God's truth for all of God's people. And as pastors, they consistently kept in view the fourfold purpose (or use) for which Scripture was given—namely, "for doctrine, for reproof, for correction, for instruction in righteousness" (2 Tim. 3:16).

In J. I. Packer's words, the Puritans "were men of outstanding intellectual power, as well as spiritual insight. In them mental habits fostered by sober scholarship were linked with a flaming zeal for God and a minute acquaintance with the human heart. All their work displays this unique fusion of gifts and graces."[1] This is especially evident in *The Cure for Unjust Anger*, this newly titled modernization of John Downame's practical treatise, first published in 1600 as *Spiritual Physick to Cure the Diseases of the Soul, Arising from Superfluitie of Choller, Prescribed out of God's Word*.

Downame belonged to the earlier generation of Puritans and is lesser known today than those of the mid-seventeenth century, such as Richard Baxter, Thomas Watson, and John Owen. He was born in 1571 during the reign of Elizabeth I, educated at Christ's College, Cambridge, and served as both a vicar and rector from 1601 to 1618. He did not marry until 1623, when he was wed to the widow of Thomas Sutton, Catherine, with whom he had seven children. A popular preacher as well as an editor and a licenser of books, Downame was also involved in examining candidates for ordination.

Downame died in London in 1652, having authored ten books, including a Bible concordance; several practical treatises on the sins of lying, swearing, drunkenness,

---

1. J. I. Packer, *The Quest for Godliness: The Puritan Vision of the Christian Life* (Wheaton, Ill.: Crossway, 2012), 29.

whoredom, and bribery; lectures on the first four chapters of Hosea; and his most famous book, *The Christian Warfare*, published in four parts from 1609 to 1618. But his short, diagnostic manual on "choller" (that is, anger) was his first. According to Packer, "Downame stands with Perkins, Greenham, and Richard Rogers as one of the architects of the Puritan theology of godliness."[2]

The Value of This Book
Downame's treatise on anger is a brief, but valuable book marked by three features: clarity, practicality, and piety.

Clarity
Readers will quickly note that Downame approaches his topic with a methodical, analytical mind. The great physician-turned-preacher D. Martyn Lloyd-Jones often spoke of the importance of moving from the general to the specific when analyzing a problem. Downame takes a similar approach. As a skilled physician of souls, he begins by carefully defining anger and distinguishing righteous anger from that which is unjust (chapters 1–3). He then proceeds to consider the properties, causes, kinds, and effects of unjust anger (chapters 4–8). Then he prescribes remedies for the cure of sinful anger

---

2. As quoted in Joel Beeke and Randall J. Pederson, *Meet the Puritans: With a Guide to Modern Reprints* (Grand Rapids: Reformation Heritage Books, 2007), 188. For a brief biographical sketch of Downame, see pages 187–89 in *Meet the Puritans*.

by marshaling out practical strategies for both preventing and overcoming unjust anger in its different forms (chapters 9–12). As I worked through these chapters, I could not help but think of people who would greatly benefit from reading them. And as these chapters worked through me, I could not help but be convicted of my own sins in the realm of anger.

Practicality

I've already hinted at the practical value of Downame's treatise, but allow me to say two more things. First, Downame writes as a skilled practitioner who has assembled a comprehensive moral and spiritual pharmacy for treating sin-sick souls. His counsel bears the marks of proverbial wisdom as he ransacks the Scriptures for both principles and examples that illustrate truth. Downame knows his Bible well, freely quoting from the Gospels, the Epistles, Wisdom literature, and both Old and New Testament narratives. But not only that, he also freely employs the best stories and maxims from classical moral and ethical philosophers such as Seneca, Plato, and Plutarch. The result is that Downame writes with what I can only call sanctified moral sanity.

This leads to the second thing: Downame's incisive ability to cut through the complexities of anger and provide simple but effective strategies for prevention and cure. Some writers are so simple as to be naïve while others are so complex that they lose the forest for the trees.

Rare is the author who understands the complexity of an issue yet can still prescribe clear, actionable solutions. Downame is such an author. He knows, for example, that the body affects the mind, and vice versa. Further, his book reveals a clear understanding of the role habits play in forming character (an area that is currently receiving much attention in both Christian and secular literature). On top of this, he has a clear grasp of how relational dynamics (especially in the home) can aggravate and reveal our unique proclivities toward sin. But while he "gets" the complexity of our emotions, he is also able to clearly and simply apply the truth to the heart.

Piety

And yet Downame is not a moralist! Moral sanity? Yes. Moralism? No. Unlike so much popular psychology today (even of the religious variety), Downame is not content to simply prescribe things to do. He is not a superficial physician, and he does not heal the wounds of God's people slightly (see Jer. 6:14). On the contrary, he deeply probes our wounds, showing that the heart of anger is a matter of the heart itself—the heart that is not only *diseased*, but *dead* in sin—and in need of regeneration, repentance, and sincere faith in Christ's atoning work on the cross. Genuine change, therefore, is wholly dependent on God's saving grace. "Where there was once a corrupt spring gushing forth in polluted streams of sin into the deep gulf of eternal perdition,"

Downame writes, "now there is a fountain of life leading them to depart from the snares of death (Prov. 14:27)."[3] In other words, *The Cure for Unjust Anger* is a book not only marked by clarity and practicality; it is also marked by piety, "that reverence joined with love of God which the knowledge of his benefits induces," of which Calvin wrote.[4] It is this combination of clarity, practicality, and piety that makes *The Cure for Unjust Anger* such an exceptionally helpful book.

A Note on the Editing

The Cure for Unjust Anger is a modernized version of the original seventeenth-century book. In the course of editing, I have replaced archaic terms with contemporary words, broken down long (often paragraph-length) sentences into shorter sentences, and clarified obsolete idioms and illustrations. I have also added headings and subheadings, organized the material into twelve chapters instead of the original ten, and added explanatory footnotes as needed. Downame quoted often from classical authors, such as Seneca and Plutarch, usually in Latin, followed by his own translation. For these quotations, I have removed the Latin and have instead used English translations available to modern readers, which

---

3. See p. 70 of this book.

4. John Calvin, *Institutes of the Christian Religion*, ed. John T. McNeill, trans. Ford Lewis Battles (Philadelphia: Westminster Press, 1960), 1.2.1.

are documented in the footnotes. While I have removed a few passages that seemed tangential, confusing, or inappropriate to modern readers, I believe the work as it now stands remains faithful in both scope and substance to Downame's original book.

My prayer is that *The Cure for Unjust Anger* will be useful not only to pastors and counselors but also to ordinary believers who desire to overcome unjust anger and live in the relational harmony that is possible only through God's grace in Christ and the Spirit.

—Brian G. Hedges

Introduction

In considering the universal infection of the contagious disease of unjust anger in the soul, along with the manifold and pernicious evils it produces in both private and public, I thought it would be helpful to prescribe some remedies from God's Word for those patients committed to my care. May these remedies help either to (1) preserve them from these fever-like fits which cause people to outwardly tremble as they are inwardly inflamed or (2) calm their heated emotions if they have already fallen into sinful anger.

At first, I thought to communicate these remedies only to those under my own care. But I was persuaded by more skillful physicians than myself that publishing them might be helpful for others. Therefore, since I desire nothing more than to use my poor gifts for God's glory and the benefit of my fellow servants for whose good they are given, I have agreed to their request.

In view of this, though I had sketched only a rough, unpolished draft, I was happy to review this work, changing and adding things to make it more suitable for the press than for the pulpit. If anyone thinks I have been too hasty in this, I hope they will excuse me when they consider that I've applied my small skill not to the vital parts of the soul but to the affections, and yet the curing of the affections (or this one in particular) may greatly benefit the whole soul. Just as a disease in the feet affects the whole body, so it is when distempered affections are infected with the contagion of original sin. And just as healing the feet brings comfort to the person as a whole, so also will purging corruption from the affections bring peace to the higher parts of the soul, the understanding and will. Seeing then that great good with little danger can result from this, I have ventured to offer this cure. I am content to undergo the censure of too much haste from some who are, I fear, much too slow in these situations. My purpose is to use all my skills to benefit many.

May the Lord, who is the only true Physician for sin-sick souls, bless this and my other endeavors to make them profitable for the setting forth of His glory, the benefit of my brethren, and furthering the assurance of my own salvation. Amen.

CHAPTER 1

The Nature of Anger

Be ye angry, and sin not: let not the sun go down upon your wrath.
          —Ephesians 4:26

The miserable ruins of our excellent state at creation and the foul spots of original corruption appear nowhere in the body or soul as clearly as in the affections. These ruins are the lamentable effects following our first parents' sin, and these spots are like a contagious leprosy that has spread from them to infect all their descendants, resulting in affections so corrupted and disordered that only the smallest relics of humanity's created purity remain. And this is why the heathen philosophers plainly discerned the great corruption of our disordered affections—even though they didn't perceive how the foggy mists of original sin had dimmed and darkened the bright shining beams of reason and understanding, the excellence of which they highly extolled. In fact, some of them, swayed with too much vehemence in speaking against the affections, have condemned them as evil in their own nature and therefore to be wholly abandoned, seeing there was no hope to amend them. Others, with greater discernment concerning the difference between the affections themselves and their corruption, have written whole treatises on reforming the affections. They esteemed the ordering and governing of these disordered and tumultuous passions to be the very perfection of wisdom.

Even the heathen philosophers, walking in the darkness of ignorance and error and enlightened with only the glimmering spark of natural reason, could both discern the corruption of the affections and study to reform them, bringing them under the rule of reason. How much more earnestly should we endeavor not merely to subject them to natural reason (which is but a blind leader) but to reform and purify them by God's word? For God's word, like the glorious sun having dispelled the foggy mists of ignorance and error, has exposed the deformities of our affections far more clearly than blind reason.

We should earnestly labor to reform all our affections, but especially anger, which is the most turbulent and violent affection if not bridled and restrained. I have chosen this text to help us in this good endeavor in order to show the ways in which anger is to be approved and embraced and the respects in which it should be avoided and shunned.

In handling this text, I will first show the meaning of the words and then break them down into their various parts. And in showing the meaning of the words, I will first define what anger is, then distinguish between the different kinds of anger.

The Definition of Anger

Anger is an affection in which someone is moved to retaliation in response to a perceived injury[1] or injustice. The injury in question may be either a true injustice or only an injury in one's perception, and it may be an injury against oneself or one's friends, relatives, or some other group.

There are two Greek words for anger, *thumós* and *orgē*. *Thumós* denotes the displeasure itself, while *orgē* often suggests the desire for retaliation, the indignation directed toward the perceived injury. Together, these words contain the material and formal causes of anger: the material cause is the disturbance itself (*thumós*), while the formal cause is the appetite for retaliation or revenge for the injury (*orgē*). The most common word for anger in Hebrew is *aph*, a term that signifies the nose or nostrils and, by a synecdoche,[2] the whole face. The word

---

1. By "injury" Downame does not mean primarily a physical injury, but any kind of wrong or offense committed against another person.

2. A *synecdoche* is a figure of speech in which a part represents the whole.

suggests anger because anger is often expressed and quickly discerned through vehement facial expressions. Our English word *anger* is derived from the Latin word *angor*, which signifies strangulation or choking as well as mental distress, grief, and anguish. This is because immoderate anger often produces both of these effects, tormenting both the mind and body.

And anger is an affection, for the whole essence of a human being consists in these three things: body, soul, and affections. Anger is an affection that participates in the body and soul as well. It is not a property of the soul only, for the emotion itself arises and is felt in the body. But it is not a property of the body alone, for the affection is provoked by a perceived injury, and this more properly belongs to the soul. I therefore call anger a mixed affection, proceeding from both body and soul.

The Different Kinds of Anger

Having provided this general definition, we can now consider the different kinds of anger. First, there is the natural affection of anger, an expression of human nature as created by God. Second, we will consider this affection as it has been corrupted by original sin since the fall. And third, we will consider this affection as it is renewed and sanctified by God's Spirit.

Unlike the Stoics, we do not confuse these three expressions of anger.[3] We do not condemn all expressions of anger without making distinctions between them. For no matter how turbulent and pernicious this affection is when it is corrupted, we must hold that the natural affection itself, as created by God and to whatever degree it is renewed and sanctified by God's Spirit, is just, holy, and lawful.

We can easily prove this with a variety of reasons. First, this affection is created by God and was a part of human nature prior to the fall, before evil entered into the world. Uncorrupted human nature, being the Lord's own workmanship, was approved by God as "very good" (Gen. 1:31). It therefore follows that this affection in its own nature should be esteemed as good and lawful.

Second, anger, or wrath, is often attributed to God Himself in Scripture: "For the wrath of God is revealed from heaven against all ungodliness and unrighteousness of men" (Rom. 1:18). "He that believeth on the Son hath everlasting life: and he that believeth not the Son shall not see life; but the wrath of God abideth on him" (John 3:36). Since it is ascribed to God, and since His

---

3. Stoicism was a system of moral philosophy founded by Zeno in the fourth century BC. While Downame critiques the Stoic rejection of all forms of anger, he also favorably quotes Seneca, one of the most famous Stoic philosophers, multiple times throughout this book. It is clear that Downame rejects Stoicism as a system yet is still able to affirm the value of certain aspects of its moral teaching.

perfect and just nature agrees only with that which is just and holy, it follows that this affection itself is to be esteemed. It is true that neither this nor any other affection can properly be said to be in God but is attributed to Him only in order to help our weak capacities better understand how He exercises His works and His eternal councils toward His creatures. Nevertheless, since nothing is attributed or ascribed to God that is not good and just, so far as it is ascribed, it is evident that anger in its own nature is not evil.

Finally, it is clear that this natural affection is in itself lawful because we see it truly and naturally expressed in our Savior, Christ Himself, in His human nature. This is evident in Mark 3:5, where Jesus looked with anger on the scribes and Pharisees because of their hardness of heart. We also see this when He was provoked with righteous indignation in seeing His Father's house turned into a marketplace, which led Him to drive the buyers and sellers from the temple (John 2:13–17). Seeing then that Christ was angry and yet free from all sin (1 Peter 2:22), it follows that anger in its own nature is just and holy.

Objections against Righteous Anger

But someone might object that anger is often condemned and forbidden in Scripture. For example, in Matthew 5:22 we read "that whosoever is angry with his brother without a cause shall be in danger of the judgment."

The answer is that this passage condemns unjust anger—not the affection itself as created or renewed by God's Spirit, but as depraved and corrupted by original sin. For sanctified anger is not only just and lawful but also necessary, profitable, and commendable. It is the whetstone of true fortitude by which we are stirred up and encouraged to maintain the glory of God, as well as our own persons and states, against the impiety and injustice of people. Therefore, though anger is a bad mistress to command us, it is a good servant to obey us. Though it is an ill captain for leading our forces onto the battlefield against our spiritual and temporal enemies, it is a good soldier as long as it remains subject to the discipline and control of sanctified reason.

The Stoics will further object that anger is a disturbance of the mind and is therefore evil. To this I answer that the disturbance of the mind for unjust causes is evil. But when the mind is perturbed on just and necessary occasions, anger is just and to be commended—such as when one sees God dishonored, religion disgraced, or wickedness unpunished. If these things disturb and trouble a person's mind, this perturbation should not be condemned, but commended. In fact, we should condemn those who are *not* perturbed by evil. So we see our Savior perturbed by evil not only when God's house was dishonored (John 2:17) but also before raising Lazarus

from the dead (John 11:33).[4] We witness the same in
Phinehas when he saw the shameless sin of Zimri and
Cozbi (Num. 25:6–15) and in Elijah when God's
worship was opposed, idolatry was established, and
the Lord's true prophets were destroyed (1 Kings 19).
Therefore, though anger is a perturbation of the mind,
it does not follow that it is evil in itself, for it is not
the disturbance itself but the cause of it that renders it
good or evil.

Furthermore, when the Stoics object that anger
blinds and confuses reason, I answer, first, that when
anger is temperate and moderate, it will wait on reason, not overthrow it. In fact, it makes a person more
constant and resolute in walking the clear path of truth
rather than stumbling in the way or turning into the
bypaths of error.

And second, though we grant for the moment that
reason is somewhat disturbed with the passion, it does
not follow that this is evil or unprofitable, for before the
affection is inflamed, reason discerns the injury. Reason kindles the flame of anger. And though this flame

---

4. The phrase "groaned in the spirit" in John 11:33 (KJV) translates the Greek word εμβριμαομαι (embrimaomai), which can carry
connotations of sternness or anger. As one lexicon says, it can be an
expression "of anger and displeasure." W. Arndt, F. W. Danker, and
W. Bauer, *A Greek-English Lexicon of the New Testament and Other
Early Christian Literature*, 3rd ed. (Chicago: University of Chicago
Press, 2000), 322..

temporarily disturbs the mind, reason is not thus made less fit to discern the injury. Therefore, moderate and sanctified anger is far from hurting and hindering the judgment of reason; it rather aids and supports reason by provoking it to courageously execute what reason has resolved. Just as the most precious eye salve temporarily blurs the vision but afterward causes the eye to see more clearly, so the affection of holy anger first perturbs reason but afterward renders it more active in executing and performing that which is good.

Righteous Anger Is Commanded; Sinful Anger Is Forbidden

Having established the lawfulness of anger both as a natural affection and as it is sanctified by God's Spirit, and having seen that anger can be either just or unjust, we will now consider how Ephesians 4:26 commands the one and forbids the other.

Though the affection as created by God is just and holy in itself, the beauty and excellence of it is now defaced with the foul spots of original sin, so that only relics of its created perfection remain until renewed and restored by God's sanctifying Spirit. Therefore, the natural affection itself is not here commanded or forbidden. Instead, we see sanctified anger commanded and corrupt anger forbidden.

The words of this verse may therefore be divided into two parts. First, there is an exhortation or commandment in which just and holy anger is commended in the words, "Be ye angry." Second, there is a prohibition against unjust, corrupt anger in the words, "and sin not." And since in our corrupt state we are prone to fall into unjust anger, the apostle limits and restrains it to a short time, lest it should turn into malice: "Let not the sun go down upon your wrath." In other words, although you fall through infirmity into rash, unadvised anger, do not continue in your sin.

Some interpreters think the first words are a concession rather than a command and should be understood like this: "If you become angry, do not sin." In other words, if through your infirmity you fall into anger, do not add sin to sin by continuing in it. But I see no reason why the words should be forced into this interpretation. It is not absurd to take the words at face value. For I would simply ask whether "Be ye angry" refers to anger that is lawful and just or that which is unlawful and unjust. If it refers to that which is lawful and just, why may it not be commanded, seeing it is as necessary to furthering God's glory and our good as any other sanctified affection? If it is unlawful and unjust, as they understand, please explain how we can be angry and sin not. They object that if this referred to holy anger, there would be no need for the restraint, "let not the sun go down upon your wrath," for, they reason, the longer it lasts, the more it should be commended. To answer is simple. The words "let not the sun go down upon your wrath" refer not to the precept ("be ye angry") but to the prohibition ("and sin not"), where unjust anger is forbidden.

This then is the sense of the words: be angry and spare not, inasmuch as your anger is just and holy. But in that your righteous anger may easily degenerate and become unjust by reason of your infirmity and corruption, take heed that you do not sin by being unjustly angry. And if through infirmity you fall into this sin, do not harbor it—no, not for one day. "Let not the sun go down upon your wrath."

CHAPTER 2

Righteous Anger

Having considered the meaning of the words in Ephesians 4:26, we will now look into its different parts, beginning with just anger. We will consider what it is and what is required in our anger for it to be considered just and holy.

Just anger is a holy and reasonable desire for revenge against sin. It is provoked within us by just and necessary causes, so that being lawfully angry with sin and vice, whether in ourselves or in others, we are provoked to punish them (the sins, not the persons) that God may be glorified, the parties amended, and God's judgment averted not only from the offending party but also from the church and the nation.

Anger is just and righteous when it is occasioned by a just cause, is expressed in a godly manner, is fixed on the proper object, endures for the appropriate time, and is directed toward holy ends.

Righteous Anger Must Be Occasioned by a Just Cause

The first requirement of holy and lawful anger is that it be occasioned by a just cause, and these causes are diverse.

The Glory of God

Anger is righteous when we are provoked with a zeal for God's glory. When we see God dishonored and His glory defaced, it is both lawful and necessary for us to be angry, for we profess ourselves to be God's subjects, and surely no good subjects can endure to see or hear the glory of their sovereign king denounced. We profess to be God's servants, but can good servants abide to see their master disgraced? We profess to be God's children, and good children are more grieved and offended when they see their parents injured than if the injuries were offered to them. Therefore, if we are loyal subjects, faithful servants, and loving children, we must be provoked to holy anger when we see our glorious Sovereign, our good Master, and gracious Father in any way dishonored.

As an example, consider Moses when he saw that the children of Israel had saved manna until the next morning, contrary to God's command. Moses could not help but express this holy anger when he saw that his Lord and Master was not obeyed (Ex. 16:20). Though Moses was the meekest man on earth (Num. 12:3), he could not endure to see God's ordinance despised. In the same way, when he saw the glory and honor due to Almighty God given to the golden calf, a base, brutish idol, he was

provoked to holy anger. He was so completely filled with
divine and heavenly rage that he not only broke the two
tables written by God's own hand but avenged their idolatry with the death of three thousand people (Exodus
32). Though the people were dearer to him than his own
life, even the salvation of his own soul (Ex. 32:32), the
glory of God was more precious to him than both.

When Phinehas saw God dishonored with the
shameless sin of Zimri and Cozbi, he was provoked
with holy anger and punished this dishonor by killing
both the offenders (Num. 25:7–8). Elijah was also zealous for God's glory and slew the prophets because the
children of Israel had forsaken God's covenant and cast
down His altars (1 Kings 19:14). And Christ our Savior
was also possessed with a fervent zeal for His Father's
glory (John 2:17).

Therefore, if we would prove ourselves to be God's
children, we must follow their example. As nothing
dishonors God more than sin, nothing should offend
and displease us more than sin, whether in ourselves
or in our neighbor. Therefore, when we fall into sin, we
should be offended with ourselves, that we might divert
the Lord's anger away from us. For as those who judge
themselves will not be judged by the Lord (1 Cor. 11:31),
so those who are angry with themselves for sin will
escape the Lord's anger.

Our anger then should lead to holy revenge against
sin. For example, those who have offended by gluttony

and drunkenness should discipline themselves with fasting and abstinence. Those who have wallowed in sensual pleasures should subdue and mortify their sins, even if they are as precious to them as their right hand and eye. And those who have defrauded their neighbor by stealing away their goods should make fourfold restitution like Zacchaeus (Luke 19:8).

And just as we are bound by the law of charity to love our neighbors as ourselves, so we should also be angry with them (as we are with ourselves) with this holy kind of anger against sin. So whenever we see them dishonor God through sin, we should be displeased and, as the limits of our callings allow, show ourselves offended. We see this in the example of the prophet Jeremiah, who was filled with the Lord's fury when the people refused to hear the word of the Lord (Jer. 6:10–11).

But our lamentable experience shows that zeal for God's glory is cold in this age frozen in the dregs of sin. For who are angry in this way with themselves because by their sins they have dishonored God? People show their tempers when their sins receive fitting punishment but treat themselves mildly, with no bitterness. An adulterer regrets his sin if he is required to appear in a white sheet, though the poison of his sin is sweet to his envenomed appetite.[1] The covetous extortioner

---

1. In the seventeenth century, the offense of adultery was sometimes punished by having the culprits wear white sheets in front of the parish congregation. See John Turner, "Penance in a White

is greatly offended if he is justly deprived of the riches he has unjustly gained, but he is not angry with the sin into which he has fallen. When a blasphemer is merely reproved for his blasphemy, he is enraged but is not displeased with himself for dishonoring the majesty of God, even though by the law of God he deserves death. In a word, everyone is angry with final punishment, though unmoved by their greatest sins. But if we would be angry and sin not, we should be less displeased with the punishment we've incurred and justly deserve than by the way we have dishonored God by our sins.

Similarly, we have misused our anger toward others. People are quickly stirred to anger against their neighbors over every little occasion and injury, even if just an unkind word or strange look. But when God is dishonored, His name blasphemed, His religion denied, His Sabbaths profaned, and His whole worship despised, people look on the offenders with a smiling face and confirm them in their sins. Or, if they are angry, they either never show it or show it in such a cold manner that it is hardly noticed. But if they suffer the least injury, there are no limits to their fury! But if we would show ourselves to be God's children and servants, we must be as zealous for His honor and glory as for our own reputation.

Sheet," *First Things*, June 20, 2013, https://www.firstthings.com /blogs/firstthoughts/2013/06/penance-in-a-white-sheet.

Unjust Personal Injury

The second cause of righteous anger is injury offered to a person's self. God's law requires us to seek the preservation of our own good name and state; therefore, when either is violated or questioned, we may justly use holy anger to aid in defending ourselves, resisting injury, and even in seeking fitting restitution by pursuing justice according to the laws of the land.

We can provide many examples to prove this point. Though Moses was the meekest man alive, when he was reviled by Korah and his companions, he became very angry and asked the Lord not to respect their offerings. The apostle Paul was a man of admirable patience, but when the high priest commanded him to be struck unjustly, Paul showed his anger with a sharp reproof (Acts 23:2–3). Even our Savior, the living picture of true patience, when unjustly struck by the servant of the high priest, reprimanded him (John 18:23)—though He at the same time offered Himself to suffer, as it were, all the scornful injuries that pride or malice could imagine or impose.

Someone might object that our Savior taught us to turn the other cheek. But Christ did not mean that we should expose ourselves to all injuries but should rather refrain from personal revenge. He would have this so far from us that we should be prepared to receive a new injury rather than take vengeance into our own hands.

The Unjust Injury of Others

The third cause of righteous anger is when our family, friends, and neighbors are injured. For since we are bound by the law of charity to love them as ourselves, so we are bound to be angry for their injuries, as if they had been our own.

This is why Moses was angry with the Egyptian who wronged the Israelite (Acts 7:24). David was angry with Amnon for raping his sister and with Absalom for murdering Amnon (2 Sam. 13:1–21). In the same way, good Nehemiah was provoked to anger when he saw the people oppressed (Neh. 5:6). This anger is not only lawful but necessary. The neglect of this anger is a grievous sin in God's sight. We can see this in the example of Eli, for when his sons took advantage of the Lord's people, Eli failed to show anger in correcting them, aside from mild admonitions. His indulgence provoked the Lord to inflict a heavy punishment. As Bernard comments, "Because Eli's anger toward his sons was lukewarm, God's anger against him waxed hot as fire." And this was just, for as Gregory says, "Not to be angry when just cause is offered is to null the amendment of sin; and not to hinder sin when a man has good opportunity and a lawful calling is to become an accessory to sin."[2]

---

2. Bernard of Clairvaux (1090–1153) was a French abbot and leader in the twelfth century noted for his quest to reform monasticism, his founding of the Cistercian order, and his sermons on the Song of Songs. Gregory the Great (540–604) was pope of the

And as they sin against the injured party, so they sin against the person who does the injury. For by not showing themselves offended, they give approval. And by giving approval, they encourage and confirm him in his sin. But if they showed their displeasure, it might be a means for reclaiming him by working into his heart a consideration of the offense for which he is reproved. In this respect, Solomon says, "Anger[3] is better than laughter: for by the sadness of the countenance the heart is made better" (Eccl. 7:3).

The Cause of Righteous Anger Must Be Serious

We have considered the causes for righteous anger, but there is a further requirement: not only should the cause itself be just but also serious and of some importance. If every trifle were sufficient to provoke us to anger, we might well show great justice, but we would without question show little love. For love is longsuffering, not easily provoked, endures all things, and covers a multitude of sins (1 Cor. 13:4–7; 1 Peter 4:8). How little love must people therefore have if they get angry for every small, trifling occasion, however just it may be! Therefore, before we loosen the reins on anger, let us consider

---

Roman Church in the late sixth and early seventh centuries, dubbed by Calvin as "the last bishop of Rome" (*Institutes*, 4.17.49). Downame did not include sources for his quotations from Bernard and Gregory.

3. Or "sorrow." "Anger" is the marginal reading in the King James Version.

not only the justness of the cause but also whether it is light or weighty. If we find that it is only a trifle, we should either wisely conceal or mildly pass over the offense, knowing that in many things we all offend. If the offense is serious, then it is not only just but also necessary to show anger; for it is no less a sin to show mildness when the Lord requires anger than to show anger when He requires mildness.

Righteous Anger Must Be Expressed in a Godly Manner

Having considered the causes of righteous anger, we will now speak of the second requirement, the godly manner in which it must be expressed. We will look at three rules concerning this manner.

Use Moderation

The first general rule to be observed is that we use moderation, lest we mingle with righteous anger corrupt and carnal anger, causing it to degenerate into fleshly anger and then fury. Let us therefore imitate the Lord Himself in our anger, for in wrath He remembers mercy. On the one hand, we should not be so carried away with the violence of anger that in the meantime we forget love. On the other hand, we should not, like Eli, be overly mild when God's glory or our neighbor's good requires us to show just anger. When we approve of sin for the sake of the offender, we make ourselves accessories to the sin and thus subject to the punishment. We must avoid both these extremes for our anger to be just and holy.

Neglecting moderation causes many people to fall into sin. Some people think they can lawfully show all violence and fury in their affections as long as they cover their deformed anger with the fair mask of a just cause. Let such people know that even though the cause of their anger may be just, they sin against the rule of love in their manner. In this they may be compared to cruel hangmen who, though they have a just cause to execute their office (following the verdict and sentence of the court), yet do so with barbaric cruelty. So it is with those who seem glad for the occasion to show their rage and fury against the sins of their brothers and sisters. No matter how much such people pretend to be just, when the mask is removed, nothing but hatred and malice will be seen behind their fair disguise. For when their friends commit far more notorious offenses, those who choked over a small gnat will find room in their conscience to swallow a pill of sin as big as a camel, as long as it is covered with the sugar of "friendship."

On the other hand, some people with the pretense of mildness and patience are content to hear God dishonored, His servants scorned, and religion disgraced. But cursed be the mildness that causes us to betray God's glory and truth by holding our peace and winking at those who offend. Such people are so mild and modest in defending God's cause that they blush to speak a word of disapproval toward sin. But when their own reputation is criticized, they swell with anger. What is this if not too much self-love, with too little love for God? This mildness is the bastard child of pride, the mother of evil. It causes them to seek courtesy and the praise of men by betraying the glory of God.

Observe Humility and Love

The second rule is that we observe Christian humility and love in abstaining from malicious and wicked words or unjust, spiteful actions in expressing our anger. To this end we must always remember of what spirit we are. For there is no doubt that however just our cause may be, if we defend it with spiteful, bitter words, it is not God's Spirit who speaks in us. Let us rather follow the example of Christ our Savior (John 18:23), who reproved those who abused Him with great mildness; or like Michael the archangel, who, when he strove with the devil himself about the body of Moses, dared not blame him with cursed speaking, "but said, The Lord rebuke thee" (Jude 9).

Show Dignity and Respect

The third rule is to show suitable dignity and respect. There must be dignity and decorum in the one who is provoked to anger, and this must be expressed toward the person with whom he or she is angry.

Behavior should be fitting to a person's place and calling. For example, magistrates should show anger not only in countenance and words but also in their acts. A father should not show displeasure toward his rebellious children only with mild admonition but also with discreet correction. On the other hand, sometimes it is unlawful to express anger with more than words. A private citizen, for example, though rightly angry with the sin of a magistrate, should still show respect to the magistrate's office. In the same way, a son is bound to show honor and respect to his father, even though he is right to hate his father's sin.

We see this exemplified in the saints. Moses was a magistrate to whom the sword of justice was committed. When he was provoked to anger by the sin of the people, he not only showed his anger in countenance or with a mild admonition but unsheathed the sword of justice and swiftly punished the offenders for their atrocious idolatry (Ex. 32:27). John the Baptist had authority to use only the sword of the Spirit. When he was offended by the hypocrisy of the scribes and Pharisees, he expressed his anger with sharp and vehement reproofs (Matt. 3:7–12). Jacob showed his anger toward Laban, his churlish father-in-law, with mild and gentle admonitions (Gen. 31:36). Being justly incensed by the barbaric tyranny of his merciless father, Jonathan signified his anger only by rising from the table and departing (1 Sam. 20:34). Although the three Hebrew children abhorred with godly zeal the profane idolatry of the king, they showed their displeasure in humble, respectful words (Dan. 3:16–18). And even though Paul detested the heathenism of Festus and Agrippa, he showed them due respect, as fit their high callings (Acts 25). These examples show that we are to use Christian decorum and discretion if we want our anger to be approved as just and holy.

Righteous Anger Must Be Fixed on the Proper Object

Righteous anger must also be fixed on the proper object, which must not be on the person of our neighbors but on their vice, sin, and injustice. For though we should be angry at (and even hate) the vices of people, we must love their persons, and in the midst of our anger seek their good, especially the salvation of their souls. In this regard, we should grieve more for their sins than for the injuries their sins have caused. We see this with holy David, whose zeal consumed him because his enemies had forgotten God's word (Ps. 119:139). And such was the anger of Christ our Savior, who was not only angry but mourned for the hardness of the Pharisees' hearts (Mark 3:5). But we should also take heed to not show approval of sin for the offender's sake. For we ought to hate sin in our friends, our family, and in our own hearts—or wherever else we find it. In no circumstances should we love this deadly poison, even if it is brought to us in a vessel of gold, precious in our eyes.

Therefore, we must avoid two extremes: one is to hate the person for the sin's sake; the other is to love the sin for the person's sake. On the one hand, we would condemn the folly of someone who hated an exquisite portrait because it had a smudge of dirt on it—or of someone so excessively fond of the rare workmanship that they loved the stain itself! On the other hand, we would commend the wisdom of someone who liked the picture while disliking the defects. In like manner, people are foolish who direct their anger toward a person formed in God's own image because the image is stained with sin, or who approve of the filthy corruptions that deface God's image. But they are truly wise who hate the stains of sin but love the excellent workmanship of God and esteem it so highly that they are displeased with the pollution that deforms it.

But the practice of the world is far different. For people will hardly befriend a person without befriending their sins as well. Nor will they be enemies to sin without maligning the person or, even worse, hating the person while loving their vice.

Righteous Anger Must Endure for the Appropriate Time

The fourth thing to be considered in righteous anger is its time, which must be short. Though it is not unlawful to continue in anger if it remains just, in order to prevent our holy anger from degenerating through our corruptions into malice, it is best to keep anger short.

Even the purest wine will over time grow sour on the dregs. In the same way, our most holy anger, if retained for long, is in danger of receiving some sourness of malice from the dregs of our corruption.

Therefore, the best and safest course is to be quickly appeased, especially if the offending party shows signs of repentance for sin toward God or injury to us. For since God pardons and forgives the sorrowful in heart, let us not retain that which He remits.

Righteous Anger Must Be Directed toward Holy Ends

The last requirement for righteous anger is that it be directed toward holy and just ends. Anger is just when it is directed toward the glory of God, the public good of the church or nation, or the private benefit of those who suffer or do injury.

The Glory of God

We set forth God's glory in our anger when as private citizens we show ourselves to be God's children and servants by manifesting our hatred of sin in word or countenance, thus adorning our profession of faith. Magistrates set forth God's glory when they become His instruments in punishing sin and executing justice. Therefore, if either private citizens or magistrates devote themselves to this principal end in their anger, it is just and holy.

The Public Good of Church or Nation

The second end is the good of the church and nation. Though this end pertains to all who are members of these bodies, it especially belongs to magistrates, who are to demonstrate anger in punishing sin not only that civil justice may be maintained but also that God's anger may be averted. God's anger hangs over whole countries where sin is approved and not punished with justice. If sin is punished by those in authority, God will not punish the nation for it; but if magistrates wink at sin and neglect their God-given duty, the Lord will take the sword of justice into His own hands and punish not only the offending malefactor but the neglectful magistrate, and indeed the whole nation that is stained and polluted with their sins.

There are many examples in God's Word. God sent a grievous plague among the people when Zimri and Cozbi sinned, but when Phinehas executed justice by slaying the offenders, the plague ceased (Numbers 25). For the sin of Achan, God took away the people's hearts so that they fled and some fell before the men of Ai, but when the malefactor was justly punished, God's anger was appeased (Joshua 7:26). When the Benjamites failed to punish the sin of those who shamelessly abused the Levite's concubine, we know what followed: God's heavy judgment fell not only on the offenders but, with few exceptions, on the whole tribe (Judges 19). Therefore, if magistrates desire to avert the Lord's anger from themselves and the nation, they must show their anger in punishing sin. But if by drawing the sword of justice against iniquity they devote themselves to the good of the church and the nation, their end is just and holy, as is their anger.

The Private Benefit of Those Who Suffer Injury

The third end of righteous anger is the good of the party who has suffered injury. For when private citizens reprove them sharply or magistrates punish them severely for their offense, this is how the offenders are restrained from committing the same sin again. But they will redouble their injuries against others if they are not reproved and punished for their sins.

The Private Benefit of Those Who Do Injury

The last end is the good of the person who provokes us to anger by his or her injury. Private citizens should be angry with their neighbors, not to malign or seek their hurt but to discourage them in their sin and cause them to amend their ways. In the same way, magistrates must show anger in punishing offenders, not to exact personal revenge but to seek their good by reforming their vices. For what greater good can a person do for a brother than to reclaim him from the sin that would otherwise destroy both his body and soul?

But how do we seek someone's good when he or she is guilty of a capital offense? In these cases, the public good of the nation outweighs the private benefit of the offender. An offense deserving death should be punished with death so that the burden will not rest on the land. But offending parties receive benefit when the pain of punishment brings them to see and repent from their sin. Without this, they would continue desperately in their sins and so cast away both body and soul. Therefore, to prevent and cure this desperate disease, it is necessary to apply a desperate remedy and to destroy the body, so that body and soul may both be saved.

These are things required in righteous anger. If we observe these, our anger will be not only lawful but also necessary for setting forth the glory of God and the good of ourselves and our neighbors.

CHAPTER 3

Unjust Anger

Having addressed the first part of my text, in which righteous anger is commanded, I will now speak of unjust anger, which is forbidden in the words "and sin not." In other words, do not sin by falling into corrupt and unjust anger.

The Sinfulness of Unjust Anger

This vicious affection is not only condemned in Ephesians 4:26 but in other verses as well: "Let all bitterness, and wrath, and anger, and clamour, and evil speaking, be put away from you, with all malice" (Eph. 4:31). "But now ye also put off all these; anger, wrath, malice, blasphemy, filthy communication out of your mouth" (Col. 3:8). In Galatians 5:20, wrath is reckoned among the works of the flesh for which people will not inherit the kingdom of God.

Anger is also forbidden in the sixth commandment under the name of murder, both because it is the chief motive that moves people to commit murder and also because it is murder in the heart. Unjust anger is thus truly murder in God's sight, for God regards the heart more than the hands. A person may be innocent before God even if his hands have slain his neighbor if it wasn't the intention of his heart. We see this in the law where cities of refuge were appointed by God's own commandment for such cases. But if a person's intent was to harm his neighbor (which unjust anger always intends), even though his hands are free from the act, he is guilty of murder in the sight of God.

This is what Christ teaches in His exposition of the sixth commandment in Matthew 5:21–22:

> Ye have heard that it was said of them of old time, Thou shalt not kill; and whosoever shall kill shall be in danger of the judgment: but I say unto you, That whosoever is angry with his brother without a cause shall be in danger of the judgment: and whosoever shall say to his brother, Raca, shall be in danger of the council: but whosoever shall say, Thou fool, shall be in danger of hell fire.

It is evident from these texts that anger is forbidden and condemned as a great sin and therefore is to be avoided as a most dangerous enemy to the health of our souls.

The Universality of Unjust Anger

That we may exercise more vigilant care against unjust anger, consider further how this vice infects all people through natural corruption. There are no people, whether young or old, wise or foolish, or male or female, who do not carry this fire in their heart. Therefore, unless we quench this fiery dart of Satan with the water of God's Spirit and the shield of faith, we are in danger of being burned. "Can a man take fire in his bosom, and his clothes not be burned?" (Prov. 6:27).

The Violence of Unjust Anger

We will more clearly see the danger of this affection if we consider its violence, for few affections are as strong and as difficult to subdue as anger.

Love is stronger than death (Song 8:6), but once anger is allowed, it easily overcomes love. For anger can subdue any love, no matter how sincere. The father in his anger forgets to love his child, and the child his father. Anger will cause a husband and wife to neglect the duties of love and bring forth the fruits of hatred. It even makes people forget to love themselves, as we see with those who put themselves at risk of imminent death in order to satisfy their anger.

Anger causes people to show raging violence against their friends, even those more precious to them than life itself. We see this in the example of Alexander, who in anger killed his friend Cletus, though he loved Cletus so fully he could have revenged his murder only by putting himself to death.[1] Therefore, as we cannot discern the

---

1. Plutarch, *The Life of Alexander* 51.6, in vol. 7, *Plutarch's Lives: Demosthenes and Cicero, Alexander and Caesar*, trans. Bernadotte

heat of the sun when we are near a scorching fire, so the heavenly heat of divine love is not felt when the furious flame of anger is kindled in our hearts.

Covetousness is also a strong and violent vice that almost nothing can vanquish but death. Those who are possessed with it love their riches more than their own lives. We see this in the cases of those who commit self-murder when deprived of their wealth. Riches are considered even more valuable than the soul, as we see in those who fall into outrageous sins, thus plunging their souls headlong into hell in order to get momentary riches. We also see this in those who despise the means of their salvation, choosing instead some small worldly trifle. Yet anger once allowed overcomes covetousness. This is evident in the example of those who to satisfy their furious anger by killing enemies are willing to forfeit their goods. Or consider those who are provoked by anger to seek revenge and spend all their wealth in prosecuting lawsuits of little or no importance in order to impoverish those who have offended them. They pull their house down on their own heads in order to crush someone else under the weight of the ruins.

Fear is another affection of no small force and violence, for it often compels people to thrust themselves into imminent dangers in order to avoid other dangers,

Perrin, Loeb Classical Library, no. 99 (Cambridge, Mass.: Harvard University Press, 1967), 373.

or even to kill themselves for fear of greater torments. Yet anger vanquishes fear, often causing those who would tremble to see another's wound to disregard their own death, thus turning the most cowardly fear into the most desperate rage and furious resolution.

While other affections will lead people, the affection of anger draws them. Other affections entice them, but anger compels them. Others dazzle the sight of reason, but anger makes reason stark blind. Other affections make us prone to evil, but anger casts us headlong into the gulf of wickedness.

CHAPTER 4

Internal Causes of Unjust Anger

As we have seen, the turbulent vice of unjust anger is heinous in the eyes of God, universally infects all people, and is a strong, violent affection. With this in mind, my purpose is now to define what unjust anger is; to examine its causes, properties, and kinds; and then, in view of its great danger, to prescribe the remedies by which we may cure this vice in ourselves or in others.

Unjust anger is a wrongful and unreasonable desire of revenge stirred up in us by unjust causes. In unjust anger, we do not seek the glory of God, the good of neighbors, or of ourselves. Instead, our anger is expressed in an immoderate and unrighteous manner toward those with whom we should not be angry.

That unjust anger is a desire of revenge is so evident that it needs no proof. By daily experience we know that people provoked to anger by an injury (whether real or perceived) desire revenge. If they are injured by a scornful look, they retaliate with a disdainful countenance. If injured by words, they respond with vengeful words. And if injured in deeds, they desire to seek revenge with deeds.

But unjust anger is unreasonable, for the fury of anger often casts a mist in the eyes of reason, causing small injuries to seem great. Then, with this false perception, people seek disproportionate revenge: harsh words for a bad look, cruel blows for harsh words, and death for cruel blows. In other words, people respond according to the affliction they perceive, not the actual quality of the injury they have received.

The desire for revenge is both unreasonable and unjust because it is provoked by unjust causes. These causes can be either internal or external. Let's first consider the various internal causes.[1]

Self-Love

The first internal cause of unjust anger is self-love. When we immoderately love ourselves, we never think of the injuries and indignities we offer others, or we regard them so lightly as not worth reciting. But self-love also causes people to heinously aggravate the injuries they've received and then make huge mountains of small molehills. It causes the heart to easily perceive a wrong, keeps it busy in thinking about the perceived wrong, then eager to seek revenge by acting on the vengeful calamities the heart has invented. Self-love makes people think they are

---

1. The external causes are covered in chapter 5.

worthy of all love and honor. Then when someone does them wrong, even in a minor way, they think death too small a revenge for the great indignity they've suffered as such worthy persons! Even when they are respected less than they proudly desire or when others are rightly preferred before them, it is enough to provoke them to furious rage against not only those who disregarded them but also those who were preferred above them.

We see an example of this in Cain. When God respected Abel's offering over his own, Cain's incensed anger so inflamed that nothing could quench it but the blood of his brother (Genesis 4). We see the same in Saul, who could not endure to see David more honored by the people but was enraged with deadly anger against him—even though David's merits made him worthy of honor (1 Samuel 18).

Self-love makes people wink at the injuries they offer to others but magnify the wrongs they receive from others. Thus, small injuries seem great and provoke them to great anger. But if we thought less of ourselves and loved our neighbors as ourselves, we would not wrongly weigh the scales in our own favor nor give free rein to our anger by pursuing revenge.

Pride

The second internal cause of unjust anger is pride and arrogance. This is the fruit of self-love, for self-love is what causes us to have too high an opinion of ourselves, and this exalted opinion causes pride and arrogance, which in turn cause people to be more sharp-sighted in discerning wrong and more furiously insolent in taking revenge.

The reason for this is clear: proud people are jealous of their honor and reputation. And they are so suspicious of the contempt of others that the least injury provokes their anger and disdain. This is why proud people are so impatient with public offenses: because they wish to be respected and consider any offense a disparagement to their reputation.

We see an example of this in Nebuchadnezzar, who grew pale with anger when he thought himself disgraced in the sight of his princes and people by the refusal of the three children to obey his wicked command (Dan. 3:19). Haman was likewise enraged with fury because Mordecai refused to show him the public honor his proud heart desired. Haman was so angry that he thought death was too small a revenge for such an indignity and was willing to utterly destroy Mordecai's whole family and nation (Est. 3:5–6).

If blown by the winds of pride and vainglory, the least spark of anger can kindle a raging flame of fury over the smallest offense. But those who are humble are not provoked to anger, even when they are neglected. For their lowly heart makes them think they are unworthy of being highly esteemed. Even when they receive an injury, they are ready to think they have deserved it, either through their similar faults against others or their more heinous sins against God.

Covetousness

The third internal cause of unjust anger is covetousness, for this vice makes people desire great riches, and if their hopes fail them, their unjust, turbulent thoughts become forerunners to prepare a lodging place for anger in their hearts.

Covetousness makes people undertake great endeavors. But when they do not succeed, their hearts are vexed and become more wayward than children. Or if their covetous desires carried with the wings of ambition do not mount as high as they wish, they stoop down to the most sordid prey. Finding themselves unable to accomplish great things in the world, they meddle with every domestic trifle at home and cannot contain their anger at the little faults of spouse, child, or servant.

These people are angry abroad but raving mad at home. They are irritated with any person who hinders or does not further their prosperity, but they are full of rage toward their spouses, children, and servants.

Fastidiousness

The fourth internal cause of unjust anger is fastidiousness.[2] This is commonly a fault in women, especially in

---

2. Downame originally said, "Nice luxuriousness, or luxurious niceness." But the words *luxury* and *nice* had different connotations

domestic matters. For if you come into an overly particular person's house you will easily perceive how quickly she is incited to great anger over small matters. If the decor and adorning of her house don't meet her expectations, if her food isn't prepared in just the right way, if she finds a spot or wrinkle on her clothes, if her ears are offended by the least displeasing noise or her slightest tastes are disregarded even if by some accident, she is so enraged with anger that the house can scarcely contain her—or at least contain her loud, clamorous voice!

These fastidious folks are not only offended with injuries but even with the appearance of injuries. "When pleasures have corrupted both mind and body, nothing seems to be tolerable, not because the suffering is hard, but because the sufferer is soft."[3] As those who are tormented with gout are angry when someone merely comes toward them and they cry out at the least touch, only a show of injury moves these people to anger. And the least true injury incites them to rage and fury. Others whose minds are not so weakened by this

---

in the sixteenth century than they do today. Downame isn't thinking specifically of people given to luxury in the sense of a luxury cruise or of niceness in terms of agreeability or kindness, but of people who are overly particular; they are fastidious about possessions, dainty about food, and generally difficult to please.

3. Seneca, *De Ira* 2.25.3, in vol. 1, *Moral Essays*, trans. John W. Basore, Loeb Classical Library, no. 214 (Cambridge, Mass.: Harvard University Press, 1928), 219. The title means "on anger."

fastidiousness can casually pass over such trifling imperfections and resist anger in far more violent assaults.

If any think these trifling concerns too small for public censure, I would have them know that the lesser the occasion that provokes anger, the greater the sin of those so easily provoked. These people deserve a sharper reproof for anger that is provoked by every light, trifling cause, than if it were weighty and of some importance. No matter how small the occasions are, their sin is not small. Their sin is indeed great, seeing the occasion that moves them to sin is but little, especially considering that the same parties who are fiery hot in these trifling concerns are cold concerning God's glory and their own spiritual good. I appeal to their own consciences whether they are not provoked to more violent anger for these trifling concerns than when they dishonor God with most grievous sin or see Him dishonored by others. If their consciences plead guilty, let them rather be offended with their own corruptions than with the physician who desires to cure them.

Vain Curiosity

The fifth internal cause of unjust anger is curiosity, by which people are tickled with a vain desire and itching appetite to see and hear all things: how their friends behave themselves in private meetings, what their adversaries do and say behind their backs, or how their servants act in every corner. From this desire to know all things, they also know many things that displease them and provoke them to anger. They can thank their own vain curiosity for this. For if with the wise man they considered it their glory to pass over transgressions (Prov. 19:11), or if they followed his counsel to "take no heed unto all words that are spoken; lest thou hear thy servant curse thee" (Eccl. 7:21), they might have less cause for anger and more contentment.

But by their inquiry after every rumor and their curious prying into small domestic faults, they inflame their hearts with great anger. It is worse for your sight to read small print than large print because the smaller the print, the closer you hold the book and the harder you strain your eyes to see it, causing the small letters to look thick and run together. In the same way, an inquiry into small domestic faults provokes more anger because they are nearer to us and look thick and run together in our minds, while the greater offenses in the world are less often in view.

Talebearing

The sixth internal cause is to have an open ear to the gossip of all talebearers—along with a credulous heart to believe them. Proverbs 26:20 says, "Where no wood is, there the fire goeth out: so where there is no tale-bearer, the strife ceaseth." As wood is fuel for the fire, so the talebearer is fuel for anger.

We see an example in Saul who, after giving a credulous ear to the lying suggestions of that pickthank[4] Doeg, was so incensed with angry rage that the blood of innocent priests was insufficient to quench its heat. With brutal fury Saul killed all the inhabitants of Nob, including men, women, and children—even the animals (1 Sam. 22:19). David therefore, speaking of Doeg's tongue, compares it to coals of juniper—that is, to hot burning coals (Ps. 120:4)—because it so furiously inflamed Saul's anger. Even David himself gave ear to the false report of Ziba and was moved to unjust anger against innocent Mephibosheth (2 Samuel 16). Thus, having experience of the many evils that follow credulity and listening to talebearers, David purposes to destroy the man who slandered his neighbor (Ps. 101:5–7). This is also why James compares the tongue to a fire, for nothing more inflames the heart to furious anger (James 3:6).

Lack of Meditation on Human Infirmities

The last internal cause of unjust anger is lack of meditation concerning the common imperfections to which we all are naturally subject. For if we only considered that in many things we all offend (James 3:2) and that we have the same (or greater) faults as those we see in

---

4. A *pickthank* is a sycophant or flatterer, someone who curries favor by providing information about someone else. Some readers might recall Mr. Pickthank from Bunyan's *Pilgrim's Progress*, one of Faithful's accusers at Vanity Fair.

others, we would not be so quickly moved to anger over every trifling occasion.

But men addicted to anger usually imitate Lamia, who (as the poets say) uses her eyes abroad but puts them into a box when she comes home.[5] In the same way, angry people are too quick to see the faults of others when in public but are stark blind in discerning their own faults at home. Though they have a great beam in their own eyes, they easily discern a small mote in the eye of another (Matt. 7:3–5). The reason is because they hide their own faults behind their backs, never looking on them, but keep the faults of others in plain sight.

---

5. In Greek mythology, Lamia was a serpentine woman who had the ability to remove her eyes from her eye sockets.

CHAPTER 5

External Causes of Unjust Anger

Now we will consider the external causes of unjust anger. By these I mean all outward occasions for anger unjustly taken.

Virtuous Actions

The first is when we are angry with our neighbors for their virtuous actions. Some malignant eyes abhor nothing more than the bright beams of virtue. This is either because they think that the beauty of another's perfection makes the deformity of their vices seem uglier or because, like Satan, their fallen natures hate virtue because it is virtue.

We have an example of this in Cain, whose anger was kindled against his brother because he was accepted in God's sight as being more holy than himself (Gen. 4:5). Another example is Saul, who was incensed against Jonathan for his virtuous attitude toward David (1 Sam. 20:30). Or consider King Asa, who was offended when the prophet, as the Lord's ambassador, faithfully delivered the Lord's message (2 Chron. 16:10); or Nebuchadnezzar, who was enraged against the three children because they refused to commit idolatry (Dan. 3:13); or the Jews, who were filled with wrath when Christ our Savior expounded the Scriptures and rightly applied it to them (Luke 4:28).

These days we have too many examples of those who cannot patiently endure to hear their duties taught or their vices reproved from God's word. Nor will they abide private admonitions. But like a sick man with a raging fit of burning fever, they are ready to spite the physician who tries to cure them. These days the one who reproves sin is more likely to provoke anger than he who commits sin, and he who reproves atheism and profanity more than he who lives in these sins. Indeed, this disease is so desperate that physicians are more likely to suffer harm from the fury of their patients than their patients are to receive help and restored health by the skill of the best physician!

Imaginary Offenses

The cause of our anger is unjust when it is only imaginary, having no other ground than our own suspicion. Eliab was thus angry with his brother David because he suspected him to be proud, but really it was his own pride that caused the suspicion (1 Sam. 17:28). This is the most common cause of anger in these days, for lack of love causes people to assume the worst of others. Then they grow angry upon their false perceptions.

A man is angry because he waves at his neighbor, but his neighbor doesn't wave in return. Perhaps he didn't even see him or at least was preoccupied and didn't observe him. Another person is offended when her friend laughs, assuming that her friend is making fun of her. Still another grows sad by imagining that his acquaintances despise him. In a word, the causes of unjust anger are as innumerable as people's suspicions.

Indeed, people are so prone to invent causes for anger where none truly exist that sometimes they are upset when they receive small benefits that fall short of their expectations or that are less than they've seen given to others. Then they are provoked to anger with small gifts, as though they had received great injury! Let us be ashamed of such follies and learn to leave them. Has your friend given more to another than to you? Maybe the other person deserved more. Even if that person didn't, you would be content with what you received if you made no comparisons. "That man will never be happy whom the sight of a happier man tortures."[1] Has your friend given you less than you hoped for? Perhaps you hoped for more than you deserved or more than your friend could conveniently give. But if you would not be ungrateful, then consider what you have received rather

---

1. Seneca, *De Ira* 3.30.3, in vol. 1, *Moral Essays*, 329.

than what you have not received. Consider how you have been preferred before others rather than those who have been preferred before you.

Small Offenses

The cause of our anger is also unjust when we are provoked by every small and trifling occasion. It violates love and charity when every slight thing incenses us to anger, for love suffers all things (1 Cor. 13:7). Love is therefore small in the person who will suffer nothing. Love covers a multitude of sins (Prov. 10:12; 1 Peter 4:8). Therefore, those who find causes for anger where they are not instead of covering them where they are plainly show their lack of love and their great proneness to anger. It is the nature of love to make great faults seem little and little faults seem like nothing at all. But anger makes every small slip a capital offense and every disgraceful word worthy of a stab. When we behold the sun rising through thick clouds of fog, it seems larger than when the air is pure and clear. So when the foggy mists of anger overshadow reason, every fault seems greater than it would appear if this turbulent affection were dispelled with the lively heat of ardent love.

Some people are angry at others' natural imperfections, which are beyond their power to change. These should provoke compassion more than anger. Others are angry at faults committed without knowledge—unwillingly and unwittingly. But that is as reasonable as being angry with a traveler for losing his way or with someone stumbling in the dark or losing his footing, or with a blind man who walked right into you. For as the lack of sight causes a person to stumble, so ignorance (which is blindness in the mind) causes some unknowingly to offend. To be angry with them is like getting angry at sick people because they are sick! For what is ignorance if not the mind's malady and sickness?

But the whole heart that is seasoned with true wisdom is not easily provoked with faults of ignorance, unless it is willful or extremely reckless, considering that while we continue in this vale of misery, our minds are shadowed with more than Cimmerian darkness.[2] And therefore these small, trifling errors we fall into for lack of knowledge should move us to laughter, or at least pity, rather than provoke anger. For as we excuse the words and waywardness of little children, knowing they come from ignorance, so should we excuse those who unknowingly commit faults through ignorance and simplicity.

Finally, our anger is unlawful when we have no lawful end—namely, the glory of God, the public good of the church or nation, or the personal benefit of ourselves or of our neighbors—but rather private revenge and the satisfaction of our tumultuous affections through hurting the

---

2. In Greek mythology, the Cimmerians were people who lived in a land of perpetual darkness. See Homer, *The Odyssey* 11.15, trans. A. T. Murray, Loeb Classical Library, no. 104 (Cambridge, Mass.: Harvard University Press, 1945), 387.

person with whom we are displeased. This is always the case in all examples of unjust anger, such as Cain's anger toward Abel, Saul's anger toward David, Nebuchadnezzar's anger toward the three children, and the scribes' and Pharisees' anger toward Christ our Savior.

CHAPTER 6

The Properties of Unjust Anger

Having considered the internal and external causes of unjust anger, we now turn to its properties.

Lack of Moderation

The first property of unjust anger is its lack of moderation, for though our anger has never so just a cause, yet if it grows violent and turns from anger to wrath and fury, it is unjust. For unlike the Spirit of God, who is merciful and easy to be entreated, such anger is of the flesh and its corruption. This is why wrath (that is, violent anger) is numbered among the works of the flesh. And those who do these works shall not inherit the kingdom of God (Gal. 5:20–21).

We can discern whether our anger is immoderate, for it is easily known by its fruits. Anger is immoderate when it provokes us to speak words that dishonor God in any of the following ways: by blaspheming His holy name; by wicked cursing and imprecations, in which we call on God to act in accord with our malice;

or by scornful words to our neighbors, as when our anger bursts out into bitter, reviling words that tend only to our neighbor's disgrace. We see an example of this in Shimei, who bitterly reproved David for his sins (2 Sam. 16:5–8). Shimei's words clearly show that his anger sprang not from hatred for David's sin, but rather hatred for David himself.

We also see a lack of moderation when we show no regard for dignity and order in respect toward ourselves or those with whom we are angry. We see this disregard for decorum in ourselves when as private citizens we take vengeance into our own hands, for vengeance belongs only to God and to the magistrate who is the Lord's deputy. As we read in Romans 12:19: "Avenge not yourselves, but rather give place unto wrath: for it is written, Vengeance is mine; I will repay, saith the Lord." Those who take vengeance into their own hands, having no lawful calling or right to do so, violate God's ordinance. They take for themselves one of God's royal privileges and thus make themselves guilty of high treason against God, just as those who usurp the royal prerogatives of an earthly prince are guilty of treason against him.

Anger is also immoderate when we have no respect for the person with whom we are angry. For example, consider a son who is provoked to anger against his father, even if for a just cause, but who fails to show his father the honor and respect his father is due but bursts out with insolent words. This is quite contrary to the good example of Jacob, who in anger did not forget his duty but used moderation and discretion with his father-in-law, Laban (Gen. 31:36); and of Jonathan, who though he had just cause to be angry with his father, Saul, showed it by leaving the table and departing (1 Sam. 20:34). This same principle applies to a servant's anger toward his or her master, a subject's anger toward the magistrate, and of all inferior persons toward their superiors. Though we are bound by God's law to be angry for just cause, yet we are also bound to moderation and discretion, for God's law leads to order, not confusion.

Directed toward Persons Rather than Sins

The second property of unjust anger is seen in respect of its object, for as righteous anger opposes itself only against sin and injustice, so unjust anger is incensed against the person who offends—indeed, often against those who are innocent.

But if we are to be Christ's disciples, we must follow His teaching and example. His teaching is, "But I say unto you, Love your enemies, bless them that curse you, do good to them that hate you, and pray for them which despitefully use you, and persecute you; that ye may be the children of your Father which is in heaven" (Matt. 5:44–45). Christ here plainly implies that those who do not love their enemies are not the children of God. We must also follow His example, for while on the earth He prayed for His enemies when He was subjected to their outrageous injuries (Luke 23:34).

But many people are incensed not only against their enemies, who are human beings like themselves, but also against animals, as we see in the example of Balaam (Num. 24:10). Sometimes people are even angry with things that lack both sense and life, as Xerxes was angry with the rivers and sent letters full of menacing threats to the mountains.[1] We see this when people dash to the ground anything that displeases them, though they often wish to pick it up again, or when in anger they break an object into pieces, though afterward they must repay that which they have foolishly ruined. Such people may fittingly be compared to children who when they fall down beat the ground. Though they have been hurt by their own folly and negligence, they are angry with inanimate objects.

Endures for Too Long

The last property of unjust anger concerns the amount of time it lasts. When anger is retained for too long, it becomes hatred. And this happens not only when people are provoked to anger for important matters but also over trivial offenses. For when vain trifles have stirred up their wrath, they continue in it. Otherwise they may

---

1. Plutarch, *On the Control of Anger*, in vol. 6, *Plutarch's Moralia*, trans. W. C. Helmbold, Loeb Classical Library, no. 337 (Cambridge, Mass.: Harvard University Press, 1962), 109.

seem to have become angry without cause. Against all
reason they stubbornly persist in their unjust anger.
Therefore, those who retain anger increase it, that the
greatness of their anger might make others believe that
it could arise only from some just and important cause.
They thus choose to *seem* just than *be* just. We'll speak of
this later when we consider the restraint of unjust anger.

CHAPTER 7

The Different Kinds of Unjust Anger

Having considered the causes and properties of anger, we will now examine the different kinds of anger.

Two Kinds of Unjust Anger

Unjust anger can be distinguished into two kinds. It can be either hidden or open, either covered or professed.

Hidden, Covered Anger

There are two sorts of hidden anger. First, hidden anger is commendable when people labor by all means possible to subdue the affection and smother the kindled flame in order to prevent its bursting forth into unseemly words and vengeful actions. This is a fruit of the Spirit, for those who cannot prevent anger will endeavor to suppress and remove it.

But the other sort of hidden anger should be condemned. This is when people conceal the anger they nourish in their hearts in order to have a better opportunity for revenge, which they seek with such complete resolve that they refuse negotiation with the offender, lest they come to a truce or peace with one another. This anger is far worse than open anger. It is worse in respect to angry people themselves because they hide within a turbulent affection that torments them like a raging fire or a violent stream whose current is stopped. Hidden anger is also worse in respect to the objects of people's anger since the objects are less wary in preventing the other's malice and therefore more easily surprised. A secret enemy is more dangerous than one who openly shows enmity. As a small band of men lying in ambush will more easily overcome a greater force than if marched against them with their banner displayed, so weak enemies hiding their anger and watching in ambush for the best opportunity for revenge are more likely to surprise one mightier than they than if they openly confessed their malice.

Scriptural examples include the old serpent, who cloaked extreme malice under fair words and promises, pretending to be a kind friend to our first parents though he fully intended their eternal destruction (Gen. 3:1). Or consider Cain, who casually talked with his brother when he had already resolved in his heart to murder him with his hands (Gen. 4:8). Like a cunning courtier, Absalom concealed his deadly malice against Amnon, his brother, for two years. He did this to avoid suspicion, in order to gain the best opportunity for revenge (2 Sam. 13:22–23). We have a similar example in Joab, who kindly greeted Amasa, then cruelly stabbed him while he lovingly embraced him (2 Sam 20:9–10). There is also Judas, the traitor, who betrayed his master with a kiss (Luke 22:47).

Neither is our age, so fruitful in all sin, barren of such examples. For how many Machiavellians[1] live among us who will not hesitate to extend a hand to those from whom they are most estranged in their hearts or look smoothly on those against whom they have conceived the deepest malice? Their anger is like a river that is most dangerously deep in the place where its waters are most still and smooth. If you ask these people the reason for this, they will tell you (following the rules of their master, Machiavelli), "Hatred proclaimed loses its chance for vengeance."[2] Professed anger takes away opportunity for revenge, but let us remember that those who cover their malice are like the devil himself, and without repentance they will suffer the same punishment.

Open, Professed Anger

Open, or professed, anger is seen when people purposefully neglect the duties of love or bring forth the fruits of anger.

---

1. Niccolò Machiavelli (1469–1527) was an Italian diplomat and philosopher during the Renaissance most famous for his book *The Prince* and his ruthless political philosophy that justified the use of cruel, deceptive, and manipulative tactics for maintaining political power.

2. Seneca, *Medea* 155, in vol. 1, *Seneca's Tragedies*, trans. Frank J. Miller, Loeb Classical Library, no. 62 (Cambridge, Mass.: Harvard University Press, 1917), 239.

Some people in their anger are sullen and silent day after day and month after month. They refuse to speak to those with whom they are displeased, though they see them daily. It is as though they had lost not only their love and charity but their tongues as well. But such people forget that God gave them a tongue not only to sing our Creator's praise but to communicate love to one another and also to preserve love by dealing with all offenses. As the Lord has given us tongues to seek out injuries and reprove those who offend, so He has given the same tongue to help us pursue reconciliation. If you would discuss the offense with your neighbor, she would either excuse her fault or confess it humbly and seek your pardon. But when you refuse to even speak with her, you make her your enemy by destroying all means or hope of reconciliation. For what hope is there of peace if you will not even agree to discuss the problem?

Professed anger is also seen when people bring forth its fruits. These fruits are of two kinds: evil speaking and evil doing. By evil speaking, people manifest their anger in spiteful, railing words. This is unfitting not only for a Christian but also for an honest infidel! Such words are condemned in Ephesians 4:31: "Let all bitterness, and wrath, and anger, and clamour, and evil speaking, be put away from you, with all malice." That we may abstain from this hateful vice, remember that God made the tongue to be the instrument of His praise, not to dishonor Him by cursed speaking. God will not hold the person guiltless who uses this instrument He created for His praise as a cursed instrument of Satan, an instrument for reviling and slandering our neighbor. This is what Christ our Savior teaches us: "But I say unto you, That whosoever is angry with his brother without a cause shall be in danger of the judgment: and whosoever shall say to his brother, Raca, shall be in danger of the council: but whosoever shall say, Thou fool, shall be in danger of hell fire" (Matt. 5:22).

Let us also remember that by our words we shall be justified, and by our words we shall be condemned (Matt. 12:37). This is with good reason, for "the tongue is the heart's interpreter,"[3] and therefore our Savior Christ said, "For out of the abundance of the heart the mouth speaketh" (Matt. 12:34). Indeed, wise Socrates knew this well; thus, when a certain father sent his son to him in order for Socrates to perceive his character, he said to the young man, "Speak, young man, that I may see thee," showing that disposition of the heart is best known by the words of the mouth.

Seeing therefore that God judges according to the heart and that heart is best discerned by the tongue, there is great reason that by our words we should be justified or condemned. Let us also remember "that every idle word that men shall speak, they shall give account thereof

---

3. This translates the Latin maxim "verba funt animi indices." The phrase means that our words indicate the intentions of our hearts.

in the day of judgment" (Matt. 12:36). If idle words, then how much more reviling words? If these meditations were always in our minds, we would follow the practice of David in our greatest anger: we would bridle our mouths that we sin not with our tongues (Ps. 39:1).

Professed anger is expressed by evildoing when in our anger we in any way injure or seek revenge against those who offend us. These actions are both forbidden in God's Word. "Thou shalt not defraud thy neighbour, neither rob him: the wages of him that is hired shall not abide with thee all night until the morning" (Lev. 19:13). And the psalmist says that an upright person "backbiteth not with his tongue, nor doeth evil to his neighbour, nor taketh up a reproach against his neighbor" (Ps. 15:3). This shows that those who inherit God's kingdom are not to do evil to their neighbors. Consequently, those who offer injury to their brother or sister when provoked to anger can have no assurance that they are heirs of God's kingdom unless they repent. We also see this in Matthew 5:22, for if the one who uses reproachful words is in danger of hell fire, what shall we think of the one who goes further, even to wicked deeds? Therefore, as we cherish our soul's salvation, let us rule our hands even when we cannot rule our affections.

Professed anger is also expressed by taking revenge for injuries received, which is also condemned and forbidden as no small sin in God's Word. Jesus says in Matthew 5:39, "But I say unto you, That ye resist not evil: but whosoever shall smite thee on thy right cheek, turn to him the other also." Romans 12:19 says, "Dearly beloved, avenge not yourselves, but rather give place unto wrath: for it is written, Vengeance is mine; I will repay, saith the Lord."

Three Kinds of Angry People

Angry people can be distinguished into three different kinds: those who are hasty to anger but quickly appeased; those who are slow to anger but also slow to be reconciled; and those who are soon provoked to anger and stay angry for a long time.

Hasty to Anger but Quickly Appeased

The first kind of angry people is flax, which is easily kindled and set on fire but is also quickly extinguished unless the flame is continually fed with new fuel. In the same way, their anger is easily inflamed by the least spark, but they are quickly appeased, unless their anger is fed with new provocations. Their anger is like setting thorns on fire: it causes a great blaze and crackling noise but quickly goes out. So these people are quickly inflamed, but when their anger has spent itself in words (like the crackling of thorns), it is soon quenched and pacified.

In the world, this kind of person is said to have the best nature, but the truth is far different. For that nature is best which most resembles God Himself, who is slow to anger and ready to forgive (Ps. 103:8–9). Therefore, if we would really be good-natured, we must imitate the

Lord. We should be slow to anger and eager to be reconciled. As James 1:19 commands, we must be "slow to wrath." Matthew 5:25 says, "Agree with thine adversary quickly"; and that not only when you have offended him, but also when he has offended you—and that not only once, twice, or even seven times, but seventy times seven times, as our Savior exhorts in Matthew 18:22.

Rather than resting content with a hasty spirit, remember that it is condemned and forbidden in God's Word: "Be not hasty in thy spirit to be angry: for anger resteth in the bosom of fools" (Eccl. 7:9). Indeed, our Savior condemns it as murder in God's sight (Matt. 5:22).

Such hastiness to anger is a foolish vice, for as it always begins with rashness, so it most commonly ends with repentance. For after hasty people have injured their neighbor by unjustified words or injurious deeds, they are then sorry for it. They are like a foolish surgeon who first breaks his head and afterward binds it in a cast. Though this heals the wound, it often leaves a scar.

And yet these are the least evils that accompany rash anger. For how many have in their fury betrayed the secrets of a dear friend? Yes, how many through rash anger have violated or even murdered someone with whom they shared the strongest bonds of friendship? But in a single moment they commit a sin for which they will bitterly repent for the rest of their lives. There is no greater folly than this. It is thus well said by the wise man, "He that is soon angry dealeth foolishly," and,

"He that is slow to wrath is of great understanding: but he that is hasty of spirit exalteth folly" (Prov. 14:17, 29). And lest we should think that the wise man seldom sins, he also writes, "An angry man stirreth up strife, and a furious man aboundeth in transgression" (Prov. 29:22).

But angry people will defend themselves by arguing that they are naturally quick-tempered and should therefore be borne with. But we do not have this nature by creation, for we were created according to God's own image, and He is slow to anger. Rather, this corruption has taken hold of us through original sin. We should not, therefore, excuse one sin by another. Let us rather labor earnestly to have this pollution washed away through the water of God's Spirit, who by His grace reforms our sinful nature. Those who are regenerated by the Holy Spirit, though naturally as cruel and ravenous as wolves and leopards, become mild and innocent as lambs. Though they are as fierce and furious as lions, yet they become as tame as gentle calves: "The wolf also shall dwell with the lamb, and the leopard shall lie down with the kid; and the calf and the young lion and the fatling together; and a little child shall lead them. And the cow and the bear shall feed; their young ones shall lie down together: and the lion shall eat straw like the ox" (Isa. 11:6–7). This doesn't mean that regeneration takes away our nature and affections. But since it partly subdues the violence and fury of our affections and partly sanctifies and reforms them, those who once were wicked and hateful become good and useful, both to themselves and to others. For their love was once immoderately set on the world and fleshly pleasures but now is fixed on God, their neighbors, and spiritual things. Once, their hopes and ambitions were set on nothing but honors and riches. Now they long for God's presence and fullness of joy in the heavenly Jerusalem. Once, their fear of man restrained them from doing good and constrained them to doing evil. But their godly fear now curbs their unlawful desires and spurs them forward in godliness. Where there was once a corrupt spring gushing forth in polluted streams of sin into the deep gulf of eternal perdition, now there is a fountain of life leading them to depart from the snares of death (Prov. 14:27). In the same way, before regeneration, rash, unbridled anger caused me to rage against my neighbor, but that anger is now opposed only to sin and injustice that dishonors God and condemns the church and nation.

Therefore, do not excuse your rash anger by arguing that it is just the way you are. You might as well say that you cannot abstain because you are carnal and unregenerate! Those who have put off the old man and are renewed by God's Spirit have this affection partially subdued and partially sanctified, reformed, and renewed for good and necessary uses. Those who give loose reign to this corrupt affection have never been washed by God's Spirit. And as long as they continue in this state, they cannot enter the kingdom of God (John 3:5).

This excuse is no better than using Lazarus's rags to cover the deepest sores of our corruption or Adam's fig leaves to hide the nakedness of sin, which are not fit to disguise the ugly vices of anger. For corrupted nature provokes not only to rash anger but to all outrages. The murderer could as soon excuse murder by claiming that he is naturally cruel, or the adulterer excuse his infidelity because he is naturally lecherous, or the thief excuse himself for stealing because he is naturally covetous. But if a murderer or thief should argue to a judge that he couldn't help it because it was his nature, the judge would answer that it was also his destiny to be hanged. And when we are arraigned before the Lord, the judge of heaven and earth, this plea will not only not excuse us but will itself be sufficient evidence to condemn us.

Slow to Anger but Hard to Pacify

Second are those who are slow to anger, but once they are incensed are hard pacified. These are like solid timber: slowly kindled, but once ignited they burn for a long time. While they are better than the previous people in being slow to wrath, they are far worse in that they continue in it. For anger retained becomes hatred, an affection far more destructive and incorrigible than anger. For as rash anger is often followed by repentance, so this inveterate anger is usually combined with perseverance in evil. The one enslaved to this not only falls into sin but is resolved to continue in it. Indeed, he often takes delight in the sin by contemplating revenge. We see this in Esau, who resolved to retain his anger against Jacob until his father's death and in the meanwhile comforted himself by thinking of revenge (Gen. 27:41–42).

But if we would be the children of our heavenly Father, we must resemble Him not only in slowness to anger but also in swiftness to forgive. Though our brother offend seventy times seven times, yet we must continually be ready to embrace reconciliation (Matt. 18:21–22). Only then shall we "be not overcome of evil, but overcome evil with good," as the apostle exhorts us in Romans 12:21. But if we continue in malice we make ourselves like Satan—and subject to God's wrath. "For with what judgment ye judge, ye shall be judged: and with what measure ye mete, it shall be measured to you again" (Matt. 7:2). And as we forgive people their trespasses, so will our heavenly Father forgive us (Matt. 6:14–15).

Quick to Anger but Slow to Reconcile

The third type of people who are unjustly angry are those who are easily provoked to anger and, once provoked, will not be reconciled. Such people are monsters in nature and completely opposite to the Lord. For while He is slow to anger and quick to forgive, these people are slow to forgive while being prone to swift anger.

I know nothing to which I can compare this kind of anger, for natural things cannot resemble it since it is monstrous and against the nature of all things except fallen people. The fury of the fiercest lions and cruelest tigers has a natural reason and is limited to a short while. Far worse are those who are angry without cause and without end.

Since there are no natural comparisons with which to describe them, let's invent artificial comparisons. These people are like tinder that is kindled with the smallest spark and burns until consumed. But they are also unlike such tinder, for while the burning tinder can be extinguished, their anger does not diminish. When tinder burns, only the wood (or that which is near it) is consumed, but even those who are far from these angry persons are often scorched with the burning heat of their furious passion. They are like a wildfire that easily burns everything and is most difficult to extinguish, except they are far more violent and destructive.

Nothing in the world can sufficiently express the destructive nature of this wild affection. It can be likened only to the malice of Satan, who for no just cause maligned both God and us and whose malice will never end. Therefore, unless we wish to be worse than all things natural and artificial—indeed, unless we wish to be as bad as the devil himself—we must be slow to anger and quick to forgive.

CHAPTER 8

The Evil Effects of Unjust Anger

Before we consider the remedies by which we may be preserved from this sickness of the soul and some medicines to cure us once we have fallen into it, we need to understand its danger, for it is vain to prescribe medicine if the patient will not take it. And since few are willing to take medicine unless they see its necessity, given the danger of their disease, I will now show the great and manifold evils that accompany the disease of unjust anger. Then, afterwards, I will prescribe the remedies.

The greatness and danger of this disease appear by those great evils that it works. These are both private and public. The private evils concern either us or our neighbors. The evils that concern us touch the whole person, as well as the body and soul.

Effects on the Whole Person
The evils that anger brings to the whole person are diverse.

Defaces the Image of God

As God's image especially consists in the virtues and graces of the mind, so anger overthrows them all, beginning with piety, the chief of all graces, and the sum of the first table of the law.

Unjust anger extinguishes our love for God. How should we love God, whom we have not seen, if we do not love our neighbors, whom we have seen (1 John 4:20)? And how do we love our neighbors if we are provoked to unjust anger against them over every trifling cause or for no cause at all?

Such anger also overthrows prayer, the principal part of God's worship, for if we would approach the altar to offer up the sacrifice of prayer and thanksgiving, we must first wash our hands in innocence (Ps. 26:6). The apostle Paul requires this in 1 Timothy 2:8: "lifting up holy hands, without wrath and doubting." And Christ our Savior commands that before we offer any gift to the Lord, we must first seek to be reconciled (Matt. 5:23). We are therefore unfit to pray as long as we continue in our anger. This is most clear in the fifth petition of the Lord's Prayer, where we ask to be forgiven as we forgive others. And since the Lord wants us to consider this deeply, He not only includes it in the prayer (Matt. 6:12) but singles it out from the other petitions to instruct us a second time in verses 14–15: "For if ye forgive men their trespasses, your heavenly Father will also forgive you: but if ye forgive not men their trespasses, neither will your Father forgive your trespasses."

Therefore, if we offer this prayer up to God while continuing in our anger, what are we asking the Lord to do if not continue His anger toward us? A noteworthy passage applies here:

> He that revengeth shall find vengeance from the Lord, and he will surely keep his sins in remembrance. Forgive thy neighbour the hurt that he hath done unto thee, so shall thy sins also be forgiven when thou prayest. One man beareth hatred against another, and doth he seek pardon from the Lord? He sheweth no mercy to a man, which is like himself: and doth he ask forgiveness of his own sins? If he that is but flesh nourish hatred, who will intreat for pardon of his sins? Remember thy end, and let enmity cease. (Ecclesiasticus 28:1–6)[1]

Sinful anger also makes people sin against the third commandment by causing them through impatience to fall into cursing, swearing, imprecations, and blaspheming the name of God. It causes them to grievously sin against the fourth commandment by making them unfit

---

1. Ecclesiasticus is a noncanonical book found in the Apocrypha. As Martin Luther said, these books "are not regarded as equal to the holy Scriptures, and yet are profitable and good to read." Quoted in Bruce M. Metzger, *An Introduction to the Apocrypha* (New York: Oxford University Press, 1977), 181.

for the exercises of the Sabbath, such as prayer and hearing the word, for those who are possessed with anger are disturbed and distracted with thoughts of revenge for the injury they have received. There is not a single commandment of the first table that unjust anger does not violate.

As it overthrows the virtues of the first table concerning piety, so it also thwarts the duties of the second table concerning justice, beginning with justice itself. For the first general rule of justice is that all people should be given what belongs to them. But anger makes people not only forget the good they owe to their neighbors but also oppresses them with undeserved injuries and unjust revenge.

Sinful anger also overthrows charity, or love, the sum of the second table. The general rule of charity is that we love our neighbors as ourselves. But anger, instead of performing any duties of love, causes people to bring forth the fruits of hatred. Instead of loving their neighbors as themselves, anger makes them hate them as their mortal enemies.

There is no end to the particular examples we could give, but this is enough to make it clear that the furious flame of anger consumes in us all the virtues and sanctifying graces of God's Spirit, wherein the image of God consists.

Makes Us Like Satan

While God is a spirit of love and peace, Satan's nature is full of dissension, wrath, and revenge. Satan delights in rage and fury. He is "a murderer from the beginning" (John 8:44) who provokes people to kill others by filling their hearts with wrath and revenge. The heathens were not ignorant of this, for they called these wicked spirits "furies," the authors of anger, dissension, and revenge— because they fill people's minds with madness and fury.[2]

Subjects Us to God's Anger

If therefore we retain our anger toward our brothers, God will retain His anger toward us, for as we forgive others, so does God forgive us (Matt. 6:14–15). We know from experience that people who are appointed as arbitrators to reconcile neighbors are often so displeased by the unreasonable behavior and stubbornness of one party that, though they were neutral at first, they are turned into an adversary. Similarly, the Lord plays the part of arbitrator to work reconciliation between brothers. But if either of them is too stubborn and contentious to be reconciled, what is this but refusing the Lord's arbitration and thus turning God into an enemy?

Exposes People to Contempt

People are often angry because they are disregarded or despised. But the truth is that nothing more quickly leads to contempt than unjust anger. And this is true in relation

---

2. In Greek mythology, the Furies (or the Erïnyes in Greek) were grotesque goddesses of the underworld associated with exacting vengeance. Virgil recognized three Furies in *The Aeneid*: Tisiphone, Megaera, Alecto.

not only to strangers but also to one's own children and servants. For when anger and its fruits of fighting and yelling are as common over small trifles as over issues of importance, people will disregard both, knowing there is no hope for preventing anger in either case.

Effects on the Body

Now we will consider the evils unjust anger brings on people in their different parts, beginning with its physical effects.

Deforms the Body

The human body is excellent by nature, far surpassing all other earthly creatures. But anger so deforms the body that it becomes uglier and more horrible than all creatures.

For anger makes the hair stand on end, showing the obstinate stubbornness of one's mind. It makes the eyes stare as if looks could kill. It causes the teeth to gnash like a furious boar and the face to grow red, then pale, as if either blushing for shame of folly or envy of others. Anger makes the tongue stammer, as not being able to express the heart's rage. It makes the blood ready to burst from one's veins, as if afraid to stay in such a furious body. It causes the breast to swell, as if not large enough to contain anger, which vents itself out in hot-breathing sighs. Anger makes the hands beat on tables and walls and causes the feet to stamp on the guiltless earth. As you can see, anger deforms the whole body, from head to toe. How ugly must anger itself thus be when its physical effects are so monstrous! And if anger has this effect on the body, what are its monstrous effects in the mind?

Exposes Us to Physical Danger

Anger also exposes us to innumerable physical dangers by provoking others into needless fights and quarrels. An angry person is like a wasp or bee that risks its own life in order to sting the one who angers it. Angry people are so desperately resolved to hurt their enemy that they hurt themselves. In their fury, they are so ready to revenge a small injury that they risk receiving a greater injury themselves.

Even when they are not hurt by their enemies, angry people bring harm on themselves. For even when they have no foe to hurt them, in a moment of rage they will pull out their hair or punch a wall. Their rage is an outrage against themselves. That is why Solomon wisely said, "A man of great wrath shall suffer punishment" (Prov. 19:19); for he punishes himself, even when no one else will.

Effects on the Soul

Sinful anger brings evil effects not only on the body but also on the soul.

Blinds Reason

Anger, like a dark cloud, overshadows and blinds the light of reason, temporarily depriving people of their wits. This is why we say that "anger is a short madness."[3] Anger differs from madness only in duration—except anger is actually far worse, for the person who is possessed of madness is necessarily will he, nill he,[4] ruled by fury. But sinful anger is willingly embraced. While madness is an evil of suffering, anger is an evil of sin as well. While madness thrusts reason from its throne, anger abuses reason by forcing it to choose violence and become a slave to passion.

In this respect, anger is like a cruel tyrant who after invading a nation overthrows counsel, law, and order and rules over all with force and fury. Anger, having seized sovereignty in the mind, takes away judgment, counsel, and reason. Then it rules over everything else by foolish affections and raging passions. Thus, Solomon rightly says that "anger resteth in the bosom of fools" (Eccl. 7:9). Anger either finds people as fools or turns them into fools. The reason is apparent: anger makes people so rash in thought that their resolves prove lifeless, like children miscarried before the time of birth.

We have an example of this in Simeon and Levi. Like mad men, they stained their hands with innocent blood to take vengeance on one offender (Gen. 34:25).

---

3. From the Latin legal maxim "ira furor brevis est."

4. This is one of the earliest uses of the common phrase that eventually became *willy-nilly*. Originally the phrase *will he, nill he* meant "whether he likes it or not." When used today, *willy-nilly* suggests that which is haphazard.

And Saul, for the imagined fault of one, killed every man, woman, and child in the city of Nob (1 Sam. 22:19). Not satisfied with this, he raged even against the beasts in beastly cruelty. David himself, being haunted with fury, vowed to kill not only foolish Nabal but his innocent family, though he was by Abigail mercifully prevented from fulfilling his vow (1 Sam. 25:13–35).

As you can see, anger perverts judgment, overthrows counsel, and blinds reason, making it the slave of passion and fit to execute those works of darkness to which rage employs it. As the Philistines put out Samson's eyes and made him grind in their mill (Judg. 16:21), this raging passion put out the eyes of reason, thus making it a fit instrument for plotting and devising revenge.

This clearly shows that unjust anger is one of Satan's choice means for working our destruction. As he has blinded reason with rage, he can easily lead us into the gulf of all wickedness. He is like a carrion crow that makes some silly lamb its prey and thus picks out its eyes. In the same way, to prey on the bodies and souls of people, Satan first blinds reason (the eye of the soul) with the fury of passion. Then, as we have no judgment to discern his cunning schemes or wisdom to avoid them, he easily leads us to the pit of perdition. He is like a shrewd fisherman who disturbs the water to keep the fish from seeing his net. Satan blinds reason with this turbulent affection to keep us from discerning the sins that he uses like nets to entangle us. Anger so blinds reason that it makes people unable to discern good from evil or right from wrong. Reason, as God created it, should choose what is right. But anger makes people judge that right which they choose.

Therefore, as we avoid those things that harm our eyes or, if they are hurt, use medicines fit to cure them, how much more attentive should we be to avoid the sinful anger that blinds reason? For as the eyes are the light and guide of the entire body, so reason is the light and guide of the soul. When the eye of reason is put out, we wander in the deserts of sin and wickedness like Polypheme.[5] If we rightly abhor drunkenness because it causes people to act like beasts, shouldn't we for the same reason hate the vice of anger? Like a burning fever, anger so upsets and disturbs the mind for as long as the fit lasts.

Inflames the Soul with Fury

Anger vexes and worries the soul by inflaming it with fury, for what greater torment can be imagined than a distracted mind tortured on the rack of rage? As we could count someone mad who set her own house on fire, so is the one who incinerates her soul with the raging flames of anger. For in this she torments her soul not only in this life but, apart from repentance, everlastingly in the life to come. Unjust anger is murder in God's sight (Matt. 5:22), and murderers will not inherit the

---

5. Polypheme was the one-eyed Cyclops blinded by Odysseus in Homer's *Odyssey*.

kingdom of God but will have their portion in the lake that burns with fire and brimstone, which is the second death (Rev. 21:8).

Therefore, seeing that anger inflicts the soul with the wounds of sin, and seeing that sin causes death unless cured with the sovereign salve of Christ's merit, let us carefully arm ourselves against this violent passion. Let us manfully repel this fiery dart with the shield of faith. Yes, let us so strongly curb anger with reason that no outward injury can provoke it to seek revenge. It would be foolish for a person to wound his or her own body over an offense caused by someone else. But people are more foolish who wound their souls by seeking cruel, unjust revenge.

Effects on Other People

Having considered the evils anger brings to oneself, we now turn to those it brings to our friends and neighbors.

Ruins Friendship

There has never been a friendship so inviolable that anger could not hurt, ruin, and destroy it. Hence, wise Solomon counsels us not to make friendship with an angry man (Prov. 22:24); you can be sure he will break it. Therefore, Juno's words to Alecto may well be applied to anger: "Thou canst arm for strife brothers of one soul, and overturn homes with hate."[6]

---

6. Virgil, *The Aeneid* 7.335, in vol. 2, *Virgil, Aeneid VII–XII, The Minor Poems*, trans. H. Rushton Fairclough, Loeb Classical

Provokes Further Sin

Unjust anger provokes people to commit all manner of indignity and wrong against one's neighbor, including disproportionate revenge for the smallest injuries. When incensed with anger, people will knowingly choose to take revenge on offenses that were unknowingly committed. For angry words they will give blows, for blows wounds, and for wounds death. That is why the wise man says, "Wrath is cruel, and anger is outrageous" (Prov. 27:4). Indeed, wrath not only provokes people to retaliate for small offenses but for no reason at all; for anger rages against innocent people—sometimes for the very reason that they *are* innocent. We see this in Cain's anger against Abel, Saul's wrath toward Jonathan and David, Nebuchadnezzar's rage against the three children, Herod's murder of innocent children, and the scribes, and Pharisees' hatred of Christ.

Destroys Families

Anger causes people to hurt others, but none more than those they should most love, cherish, and protect— namely, their own families. Families, since they are more closely connected, are continually subjected and exposed to their fury and outrage: the spouse to bitter words; the

---

Library, no. 64 (Cambridge, Mass.: Harvard University Press, 1918), 27. Juno, the wife of Jove and queen of the gods, is Aeneas's primary antagonist in *The Aeneid*. She summoned Alecto, one of the Furies, to incite war against the Trojans. See note 5 of this chapter.

children to furious, unreasonable correction; and servants not only to reviling speeches but to cruel stripes and blows. As someone well said, "The tokens of savage and irascible men you will see on the faces of their servants and in the marks branded upon them and their fetters."[7]

Effects on the Public

Unjust anger is the cause of all tumults, uproars, seditions, conspiracies, massacres, and bloody wars—indeed, of the overthrow and confusion of cities and nations. These are the evil effects of sinful anger on the public. Such anger incites the magistrate against the subject and the subject against the magistrate, the prince against the people and the people against the prince, kingdom against kingdom, and nation against nation.

These conflicts arise not just for important causes but for trifling issues. A furious, unquenchable fire can be kindled by a very small spark if set to combustible material. A single spark can ignite a fire, engulfing an entire city in flames. And it matters not how small the issue that inflames anger, for in a combustible mind anger is sufficient to consume whole kingdoms and nations, especially when power and opportunity are equal to the violence of the affection.

---

7. Plutarch, *On the Control of Anger*, 151. Keep in mind that both Downame and Plutarch were writing prior to the abolition of slavery and the passing of just laws for prosecuting domestic violence.

We see this in many examples, such as Simeon and Levi, who put an entire city to the sword, although their angry quarrel was with just one man (Genesis 34). Or consider Abimelech, whose fury brought destruction to the city of Shechem (Judges 9). In the same way, Saul destroyed Nob (1 Samuel 22), and Haman, in his anger with Mordecai, plotted the destruction of the Jews (Esther 3). But there is no need to labor the point, since not only Scripture but also ancient histories and even our own pasts and daily experience make this evident.

You see, then, the many evils that result from this raging disease of unjust anger, for it is not only a deadly abscess in our own lives but also a contagious plague that destroys whole peoples and nations. With what great care should we then use every remedy possible to prevent or cure such a dangerous disease!

CHAPTER 9

Removing the Causes
of Unjust Anger

There are two kinds of remedies against unjust anger. First, there are preventive remedies that preserve us from anger and keep us from falling into it; and second, there are remedies that cure us from anger once we have fallen into it. In this chapter, we will consider the first remedy for preventing unjust anger—namely, removing the causes of it.

Anger is a disease of the mind. Therefore, just as wise physicians think it is better and safer to preserve health and prevent sickness than to remove disease in a sick person, so it is better in spiritual matters to preserve the soul from vice rather than purge the vice from the infected soul. As Seneca said, "Every emotion at the start is weak. Afterwards, it rouses itself and gains strength by progress; it is more easy to forestall it than to forgo it."[1] For as the common proverb is, "There are

1. Seneca, Epistle 116, in vol. 3, *Ad Lucilium Epistulae Morales*, trans. Richard M. Gummere, Loeb Classical Library, no. 77

but twelve points in the law, and possession is as good as eleven of them." If therefore anger has taken possession, it will be difficult to dispossess it.

Anger is our soul's mortal enemy. Therefore, as we first try to keep the enemy from entering the frontiers of our country, so we must endeavor to repel anger by blocking its passage into our hearts. And as we seek to expel enemies as soon as they have entered, so we must quickly expel anger and remove it from our hearts. For if we allow anger to fortify itself, it will grow so strong and violent that we will be unable to dislodge it. During the siege of a city, the citizens provide all things necessary for their defense before the assault. Then, when enemies approach its walls, they will not find the people unprepared. In the same way, if we wish to repel anger when it comes, we must fortify and arm ourselves against it before it comes, for if it finds us unprepared, it will easily gain entrance and more easily overcome us.

Let us therefore first endeavor to use all good means by which we may prevent anger. For once it has gotten hold of us, it will easily plunge us headlong into violence and fury. It will be easier if we can prevent falling into it in the first place. For experience teaches that a man may easily keep himself from running down a steep hill while he is still at the top, but once he starts running, he can't

(Cambridge, Mass.: Harvard University Press, 1925), 333. Translated, the title is *Moral Epistles to Lucilium*.

stop until he gets to the bottom. Likewise, it is easier to abstain from running into anger in the first place than to keep from falling to the bottom of fury once we have begun. And the first remedy is to take away the causes of anger, for "upon removal of the cause, the effect is removed."[2] There are seven causes of anger.

Self-Love

The first cause of anger is self-love. Therefore, if we would prevent falling into anger, we must labor to banish self-love and to follow the rule of charity: to love our neighbors as ourselves and to do nothing to them which we would not have them do to us.

Therefore, before we let the reins loose on anger, let us put ourselves in the place of the person we are angry with, considering how we would wish to be treated if we had committed the offense. Then go and do likewise to your offender. In this way, we will not aggravate the injuries offered to us, we will not excuse the injuries we do to others, we will not throw our judgment off balance with unequal affection, and we will not be incensed over offenses that we ourselves have often committed against others.

Pride

The second cause of anger is pride and arrogance. Therefore, if we would not fall into anger, we must subdue

---

2. From the Latin legal maxim "sublata causa tollitur effectus."

pride and labor for the opposite grace of humility. Those who would be meek like Christ our Savior must learn from Him the lesson of true humility: "For I am meek and lowly in heart" (Matt. 11:29).

We would not be so easily provoked to anger on every trifling occasion if we laid aside the arrogant opinion of ourselves and our own excellence. We should, therefore, consider with Abraham that we are but dust and ashes (Gen. 18:27), and with David that we are worms and no men (Ps. 22:6). With Job we should confess, "I have said to corruption, Thou art my father: to the worm, Thou art my mother, and my sister" (Job 17:14). By the sins we have committed against God and our neighbors we deserve not only ill treatment but eternal death of body and soul. We should not then think ourselves mistreated to endure lesser injuries, seeing that we have deserved far greater.

Covetousness

The third cause of anger is covetousness. We must banish this vice from our hearts if we do not want to be overcome with anger. If we were not covetous, we would not seek or expect preferential treatment. Consequently, we would not be upset or incensed with anger because our hopes would not be disappointed so often. We would not interfere with every domestic trifle but entrust matters to our children, servants, and especially our spouse, who is a joint governor in the kingdom of the home. Then, when anything goes wrong under their supervision, we should not look so much to the mean as the supreme cause—namely, the providence of God. For if He builds not the house, they labor in vain who build it (Ps. 127:1), and if He does not bless their labors, they cannot prosper.

Fastidiousness

The fourth cause of anger is fastidiousness, yet another vice we must subdue in order to subdue anger. We should labor, then, for kind and simple homes because this encourages good hospitality and preserves peace and quietness.

Remember that our first parents, Adam and Eve, were clothed with skins—very simple attire. If we were content with simple clothing, we would not be so easily provoked over every spot or wrinkle in our clothes. If, like them, we fed on roots and herbs, we would not have such excessive appetites and finicky tastes that no ordinary food could please us. If we dwelt in tents as pilgrims, like Abraham, we would not be so fancy in decorating our houses or so angry over a cobweb. If with Jacob we made the ground our bed and a stone our pillow, with only the sky as our ceiling, we would not be so displeased with the hardness of a feather bed or uncomfortable lodging. Therefore, if you take away fastidious, luxurious tastes, you will also take away one of the most common causes of unjust anger.

Vain Curiosity

The fifth cause of unjust anger is vain curiosity—the desire to see and hear everything. To avoid anger, we must abandon this troublesome companion of needless curiosity. For many things will neither grieve nor hurt us if we never see nor hear them. People who ask what is said about them by others, or who listen at every door and under every wall, or who bring up ill words spoken against them in secret will both upset themselves with anger and make their own faults more public. When Antigone heard two of his subjects speaking evil of him in the night near his tent, he called them and warned them to go farther off lest the king should hear them.[3] If we followed his example, our anger would not so much vex ourselves or trouble others.

Listening to Talebearers

The sixth cause of anger is to have ears that listen to every talebearer and credulous hearts to believe them. For it is human nature to be most desirous of hearing that which most displeases us. "We are glad to believe what we are loath to hear."[4] But if we would avoid unjust anger, we must avoid this vice as well. "We shall acquit many if we begin with discernment instead of with anger."[5] Let us not therefore suffer execution to go before

---

3. Seneca, *De Ira* 3.22.1–2, in vol. 1, *Moral Essays*, 311.

4. Seneca, *De Ira* 2.22.3, in vol. 1, *Moral Essays*, 215.

5. Seneca, *De Ira* 3.29.2, in vol. 1, *Moral Essays*, 327.

judgment but rather delay our more severe censure until time has revealed the truth. For it is most common for people to report untruths—some in order to deceive, some because they are deceived themselves, some because they wish to separate friends. Some through their accusation will pretend that we were wronged so they have an opportunity to show their sympathy for us. But scarcely any of these speak with complete truthfulness. Therefore, let us not be angry before we judge or judge before we have heard both sides. For what kind of injustice is it to listen to an accusation but refuse to hear an explanation? To pass a sentence of condemnation before we have asked the accused person what he can say for himself? What could be more wrong than to believe these things in secret and to be angry openly?

Lack of Meditation

The last cause of unjust anger is lack of meditation concerning human infirmities, either those common to all humankind or those more specific to ourselves. If we would refrain from anger, we should think often of the contagious leprosy of original sin, which has so infected all the sons and daughters of Adam that only pollution and filthiness remain within us. A person infected with the plague is not offended with someone who has the same infection. Suffering lepers don't look on the sores of their fellow lepers with scorn and anger but with pity and compassion. In the same way, when we consider this universal plague that has infected all humankind, it will not make us angry to behold the sores of this plague in others. It will rather provoke sympathy and pity and the desire to see them cured.

When word was brought to Anaxagoras that his son was dead, he was excessively moved with the news, because, as he said, "I knew that I had begotten a mortal."[6] So if we would consider and meditate on human frailty and infirmities, we should not be so distressed when they showed themselves, for this is what we would expect. We would not be so easily provoked to anger with the faults of our servants, the imperfections of our friends, and the infirmities of our spouses if we only remembered their frailties and imperfections from the start.

Furthermore, we should meditate on our own specific weaknesses and infirmities. Before we become angry with someone else, we should look to ourselves and say with Plato, "Can it be that I am like that?"[7] "Have not I also offended in this, or in that which is worse? Am I clear from offering the like injuries or greater to my brothers? Alas, no. But even if I was, how often have I provoked God to anger by my sins? And how can I seek pardon for my great debt when I cruelly exact every trifle from my fellow servant?" If we would speak like this to our own consciences in the presence of God, we

---

6. Plutarch, *On the Control of Anger*, 155.
7. Quoted in Plutarch, *On the Control of Anger*, 155.

would not so easily be provoked to anger and revenge. For we ourselves do many things that need pardon. And our greater faults, if we just considered them, might help us pass over smaller faults in others. For no one can without shame severely punish the same faults in her neighbor for which she herself needs pardon.

CHAPTER 10

Subduing Anger by Laboring for Patience

The second means to subdue anger is to labor for the contrary virtues of patience and longsuffering.

Consider God's Providence

To this end we must consider that nothing happens to us without God's all-seeing providence; He will work everything for our good if we are His children (Rom. 8:17, 28). Why should we therefore vex ourselves with anger, seeing that God will turn people's injuries into blessings? Rather, when any wrong that we cannot by just and lawful means avoid is done against us, let us say with Christ our Savior, "The cup which my Father hath given me, shall I not drink it?" (John 18:11). Should I be angry with the cup because the medicine is bitter? Or should I be angry with the hand that gives me the cup? My heavenly Father corrects me for my good. Therefore, I will not be angry with the rod, but look rather to the hand that inflicts the chastisement. I will say with David, "I was dumb, I opened not my mouth; because thou didst it" (Ps. 39:9). Otherwise I should commit as great folly as the one who is angry at the staff by which he is smitten while never regarding the one who smites.

Consider Your Sins

We should also remember that the injuries we have received are much less than our sins deserve. Such injuries are either light or, if not light, they are still momentary; but our sins deserve infinite and eternal punishment. Therefore, if the Lord uses these earthly rods to correct our sins, we should admire His mercy rather than be angry at so gentle a chastening. Let us then look on our sins, not our punishment. And so we will patiently bear the injuries of others as sent from God, who does us no wrong. Let us follow David's example, who was not provoked to anger and revenge by the reviling of Shimei but viewed him as an instrument in God's hands (2 Sam. 16:10–11).

Meditate on the Suffering of Christ

The third way to arm us with patience and so subdue anger is to continually remember Christ's bitter passion and suffering for our sins. For if we consider how patiently He endured scoffs and reproaches, railing and reviling, buffeting and scourging—yes, even death itself and God's wrath, which is more grievous than death, and that He suffered this not for any demerit in Himself but for our sakes—then we can easily suffer at our

Savior's request the small wrongs from others, seeing that we have deserved far greater (Matt. 5:39).

Those who were stung by the fiery serpents were healed by looking to the brazen serpent lifted up for this purpose (Num. 21:6–9). So, with us: if the fiery serpent of unjust anger has stung us and the burning poison of anger has inflamed us, let us cast the eyes of our souls on the true brazen serpent, Christ our Savior, hanging on the cross and suffering the wrath of God that our sins deserved. In looking to Him, the heat of our wrath and anger will soon be cured and cooled.

Consider the Necessity of This Duty

The fourth way to develop patience and prevent anger is to consider the necessity of this duty, for we have no assurance that we are the children of God if our love for our brothers is not more forceful in restraining us from vengeance than the anger that provokes us to the same. "In this the children of God are manifest, and the children of the devil: whosoever doeth not righteousness is not of God, neither he that loveth not his brother" (1 John 3:10). "Whosoever hateth his brother is a murderer: and ye know that no murderer hath eternal life abiding in him" (v. 15).

Someone might object, "I love my brother, even though I am easily angered." I answer with the apostle that love "suffereth long" and "endureth all things" (1 Cor. 13:4, 7). Therefore, those who will suffer nothing and are provoked every minute lack this love. The apostle expressly says that, in fact, love "is not easily provoked"— that is, provoked to rash and unjust anger (v. 5). Those who are easily provoked are, therefore, destitute of love.

Furthermore, it is necessary to subdue anger because while we remain angry, we can have no assurance that our prayers are acceptably heard by God. For we pray to be forgiven as we forgive others (Matt. 6:12). There- fore, if we retain our anger toward our brethren, we pray that God will retain His toward us. Not only this, but our Savior expressly tells us, "But if ye forgive not men their trespasses, neither will your Father forgive your trespasses" (Matt. 6:15), and that "with what measure ye mete, it shall be measured to you again" (Matt. 7:2). Let us remember the parable of the servant who was forgiven ten thousand talents. But after cruelly demand- ing one hundred pence from his fellow servant, he was cast into the prison of utter darkness (Matt. 18:23–35). By this we understand that if we refuse to forgive our brethren for their small injuries after the Lord has for- given our infinite and heinous sins, we will be treated like that merciless and cruel servant. Let us then follow the counsel of the apostle: "And be ye kind one to another, tenderhearted, forgiving one another, even as God for Christ's sake hath forgiven you" (Eph. 4:32).

Consider the Examples of Others

The fifth means to arm us with patience against the assaults of anger is that we consider the examples of others. Let us first consider the example of God Himself, who is merciful, gracious, and slow to anger (Ex. 34:6). As the prophet David writes, "The LORD is merciful and gracious, slow to anger, and plenteous in mercy" (Ps. 103:8). God is neither easily provoked to anger nor does His anger last for long once provoked, for "He will not always chide: neither will he keep his anger for ever" (v. 9). As soon as we knock at the door of mercy, He is ready to open it (Matt. 7:7). Therefore, if we would resemble our heavenly Father and show ourselves to be His children, we must learn to imitate His longsuffering and patience.

We should also consider the example of Christ our Savior, who is the living portrait and express image of His Father. "Take my yoke upon you, and learn of me" He exhorts, "for I am meek and lowly in heart: and ye shall find rest unto your souls" (Matt. 11:29). What was this meekness? Peter explains: "Who did no sin, neither was guile found in his mouth: who, when he was reviled, reviled not again; when he suffered, he threatened not" (1 Peter 2:22–23)—though, considering His infinite power, He was able not only to threaten but to utterly destroy His enemies. If therefore Christ, who was free from sin, was so meek and patient, how much more should we be who because of our sins deserve the greatest injuries, even eternal death?

But if these examples are too lofty to imitate, consider the patience and longsuffering of our fellow brethren. For example, when Abraham had just cause for offense against Lot and his shepherds, he yielded his rights rather than have discord and dissension (Gen. 13:8). Moses prayed for the people of Israel, even when they were ready to stone him (Ex. 17:4–11). Though David could have sought revenge against Shimei for his outrageous injuries, he restrained himself (2 Sam. 16:7–10). Or consider Stephen, who prayed for his enemies even as they stoned him (Acts 7:60).

If these examples will not move us to the love of meekness and patience, let us consider those who are subject to the fury of anger and we will easily see what a cruel and ugly vice it is. Someone said that if an angry man would look in a mirror in the midst of his fury, he would appear so horrible to himself that it would be a notable means to work hatred in his heart of such a deformed vice.[1] But angry people will hardly be brought to this while they continue in their rage. If they could be, they have already somewhat relented, and so their countenance is changed. And even if it wasn't, the fury of their affection so clouds their judgment that they justify everything they do in the moment of passion. Let us therefore follow the example of the Spartans, who would force their children to look at the Helots and slaves when they were drunk, that they might be brought into detestation of such an ugly vice when they saw its

1. Seneca, *De Ira* 2.36.1, in vol. 1, *Moral Essays*, 249.

beastliness in others.[2] Let us then set before our eyes other people while they are in their fury and consider how anger deforms the body and disables the mind. Consider the lamentable tragedies anger enacts and the follies it commits. This ugly deformity joined with cruel folly will then move us to hate such a foul vice.

Abstain from Too Much Busyness

The sixth means is to abstain from too much busyness. For the mind is distracted and disturbed with abundant busyness and thus made a suitable dwelling place for anger. Furthermore, when we are too busy, something is bound to go wrong. When too many irons are in the fire, some of them will burn and inflame the mind to anger.

Abstain from Contentious Controversy

The seventh means is to avoid contentious controversies, for "it is easier to refrain than to retreat from a struggle."[3] Once people have entered into controversy, they cannot easily give it up. For they think that it will make them look bad if they are forced to yield—even if they are yielding to the truth. People naturally desire to bring others to their own opinions, and therefore they will use great earnestness to persuade others, often even bursting into anger and fury when they fail.

---

2. Plutarch, *On the Control of Anger*, 109.
3. Seneca, *De Ira* 3.8.8, in vol. 1, *Moral Essays*, 277.

Avoid the Company of Angry People

The eighth means to prevent anger is to avoid the company of those who are angry, for people will easily be infected with their disease. And this Solomon teaches us: "Make no friendship with an angry man; and with a furious man thou shalt not go: lest thou learn his ways, and get a snare to thy soul" (Prov. 22:24–25). Furthermore, the companions of angry people are likely to be provoked by them and be burned by the heat of their flame. As one piece of wood being set on fire will kindle nearby wood, so one person inflamed with anger, by his or her provocations inflames those who are with him or her.

Bridle Anger for a Day

Finally, those who find themselves naturally prone to anger should labor and resolve to bridle their anger for one entire day, no matter what happens. And after this, let them do the same on the second day, then a third, and so on. In this way, they will gradually develop the habit of patience, and custom will alter nature.

CHAPTER 11

Remedies to Cure Unjust Anger

Having considered the means and remedies for preventing anger before we fall into it, I will now show what we should do once anger has begun and gained a foothold in our hearts. The apostle shows us this in the words "Let not the sun go down upon your wrath." That is, if you fall into unjust anger through weakness, do not continue in it. Instead, abandon this corrupt affection as quickly as possible.

We must not take anger with us to bed. And once we wake up again, we must not allow anger to wake up with us. In other words, do not treat anger like your clothes, laying them aside during the night while intending to put them on again the next day. Rather, we must put off anger as we put off the old man—with full resolution never again to entertain or assume it. We must treat anger as we would filthy rags that are not worth wearing. And this we must do not only once or twice, but every day. If the sun comes up and we have anger in our hearts, we must dislodge and expel it before the sun goes down again. And as the night cools the heat left from the daytime sun, so must it also quench the flames that anger has kindled in our hearts.

The reason he requires us to abandon anger before nightfall is because we will give place to the devil's temptations if we hold on to anger. This he implies in the following words. Having exhorted us not to let the sun go down on our wrath, he adds, "Neither give place to the devil" (Eph. 4:27). By this he notes that those who not only entertain anger during the day but allow it to lodge overnight thereby lay themselves open to the fiery darts of Satan. "Because your adversary the devil, as a roaring lion, walketh about, seeking whom he may devour" (1 Peter 5:8). When Satan finds people who have retained anger in their beds, he considers them suitable prey and comes with his bellows of fury to further inflame the fire of anger, until it flames out into furious revenge. He aggravates the injury they have received, telling them that if they put up with such indignity, they will expose themselves to more. If they allow themselves to suffer this, they will lose their reputations as well. People will think them cowards. Then, having worked into their hearts a full resolution to take revenge, he then fills their heads with the most fitting means and opportunities for taking vengeance with all rage and cruelty. And so it often comes to pass that when they arise, they will act on the very things they have desired while on their pillows.

Therefore, to prevent such great evil, if we cannot fully repel anger, let us quickly expel it. For though anger begins as only a small spark, if it is nourished, it will quickly grow into a furious flame. When a house catches fire, men labor with earnestness and speed to quench it, before the fire spreads to the main posts and great beams.[1] If they do not, it will soon be too late, once the fire has grown to its full strength. In the same way, when our hearts are first set on fire with anger, we must quickly quench it with the water of the Spirit; for once we are thoroughly inflamed, it will be too late to apply any remedy until the flame has spent itself.

But some will say, "I fall into anger many times when I never meant it, and it overcomes me before I am aware. How then can I prevent that which I do not foresee? How do I free myself from it, seeing that it violently rules over me?" To answer the first question, if we carefully watched over ourselves, we would more easily perceive when we are prone to anger. For as a storm is preceded by many signs, so we may easily discern the signs of this tempestuous storm of unjust anger within ourselves.

To the second question, I answer that anger does not rule over us as soon as it enters the heart, but after it grows to greater strength. The greatest fire has but a small beginning, and when it has just begun can be easily quenched. Similarly, the most furious anger does not immediately attain its full strength but gradually increases, like a flame taking hold of new matter.

---

1. The superstructure or framework of the house.

Therefore, though a person fully inflamed with anger can hardly be quenched, it is easy to suppress anger when it first begins. Let us then consider the means of subduing anger once it has assaulted us.

Don't Feed the Fire

The first means is to withdraw the fuel that further feeds anger. The greatest fire will eventually go out if not supplied with new material to burn. In the same way, the most furious anger will soon diminish if we don't add fuel to the fire.

The primary way anger is increased is by too much talking—the multiplying of words. For though an injury is small at first, if it is aggravated by the one who suffers the injury or defended by the one who caused it, people are incensed to great anger. In this respect, words are well said to be like wind. For as nothing causes a small spark to burst into a furious flame like wind, so nothing causes a small spark of anger to increase into a raging flame of revenge like the wind of words. We should not therefore imagine, as some people do, that we can disgorge anger from our stomachs by vomiting out bitter words. For words not only whet and sharpen our own affections; they also provoke the person with whom we are offended to retaliate in the same way, thus adding new matter to the old flame.

We can as quickly quench fire with wood as anger with words. For as wood nourishes the fire, so words are the nourishment of anger. Let us rather imitate the wise Socrates, who when he was most angry softened his speech and lowered his voice in order to withdraw fuel from the fire of anger.[2] In this way, anger will be extinguished more quickly.

Withdraw from the Company of Others

The second means to subdue anger is to withdraw from the company of other people, especially the one who has offended us. We see this exemplified by Jonathan, who, when justly provoked by his unjust and cruel father, rose from the table and departed, lest by his father's provocations he might have done or said something wrong (1 Sam. 20:34). If we imitated his practice, we would not only calm our anger by removing the object and cause of our anger from sight and also prevent further reason for increasing anger but also cover our infirmities, which would otherwise be exposed by the violence of our emotions.

Therefore, as those who because of sickness are prone to fall into fits (if they cannot by ordinary remedies prevent them) will withdraw from the company of others so that no one can witness their deformity,[3] so those who cannot curb their anger with the rein of

---

2. Plutarch, *On the Control of Anger*, 105.

3. Downame perhaps has in mind epilepsy, for which effective medications were not discovered until the mid-nineteenth and early twentieth centuries.

reason should withdraw into privacy while their fit of anger lasts in order to hide the ugliness of their vice. For fits of anger, when seen by others, often move their adversaries to scorn and laughter, and friends to sorrow and pity. This is a characteristic of a wise person. "A fool's wrath is presently known: but a prudent man covereth shame" (Prov. 12:16).

Restrain Yourself from Angry Outbursts

The third means to vanquish anger is to bridle anger and restrain yourself from bursting into revenge. For if we resist anger as soon as we encounter it, we will find its strength much weakened. The wise Athenodorus knew this well, for when he parted from Augustus, he was asked by Augustus to leave behind some good instruction for governing his empire. This was the counsel he gave: "Whenever you get angry, Caesar, do not say or do anything before repeating to yourself the twenty-four letters of the alphabet."[4]

An example hereof we have in Socrates, who, finding his anger incensed against his servant, deserved to take correction, saying, "I would beat thee if I were not angry."[5] Once when Plato was angry with his slave, he

---

4. Plutarch, *Sayings of Romans* 207.7, in vol. 3, *Plutarch's Moralia*, trans. Frank Cole Babbitt, Loeb Classical Library, no. 245 (Cambridge, Mass.: Harvard University Press, 1962), 233.

5. Seneca, *De Ira* 1.15.3, in vol. 1, *Moral Essays*, 145. Both Seneca's and Downame's quotation of Socrates reflects the times in

was unable to control himself and, bent on flogging him with his own hand, ordered him forthwith to take off his shirt and bare his shoulders for the blows; but afterward realizing that he was angry, he stayed his uplifted hand, and stood just as he was with his hand in the air like one in the act of striking. Later, when a friend who happened to come in asked him what he was doing, he said, 'I am exacting punishment from an angry man,'"[6] meaning himself by bridling his anger. If then the heathen, who had only a small glimpse of nature's light and heathen philosophy to direct them could thus defer and curb in their unruly passions, let us be ashamed to come behind them, seeing we have not only that but also the bright sunshine of the Word of God to guide us.

In order to abstain from sudden and desperate resolutions when our anger is provoked, let us consider the great danger in those moments of doing things we will regret for our whole life, for "anger is a short madness."[7] We cannot, in such a brief period, rightly examine the circumstances of the matter, which in such cases are

---

which they live, when slavery and the harsh punishment of slaves were legal. While we rightly deplore slavery today, the broader point Seneca was making is applicable: "The slave's reproof he postponed to a more rational moment; at the time it was himself he reproved. Will there be any one, pray, who has passion under control, when even Socrates did not dare to trust himself to anger?" *De Ira* 1.15.3, in vol. 1, *Moral Essays*, 145.

6. Seneca, *De Ira* 3.12.5, in vol. 1, *Moral Essays*, 285.

7. From the Latin legal maxim "ira furor brevis est."

most important. But "time discovers truth"[8] and will bring all to light. "If ever you want to find out what a thing really is, entrust it to time,"[9] for nothing is thoroughly known suddenly, in a moment.

It is a foul shame to first be angry and then to judge; to first give punishment, then to examine the cause. For then who has truly offended: the one who gave the punishment or the one on whom it was inflicted? But the truth will appear in time, whether vengeance was more justly taken or withheld. And then, if after due examination a deserved punishment is inflicted, it will be more effectual for the reformation of the offender since he or she will see that it proceeds from true judgment rather than from the spleen.[10]

When the Athenians, having heard of Alexander's death, were moved to more unbridled speeches and insolent practices, Phocine said to them, "If, men of Athens, he is dead today, he will be dead tomorrow also, and the day after,"[11] and therefore you may well deserve these curses until you are fully informed in the truth. So I say to the angry person: do not so hastily take vengeance on your inferior, for if it is a fault today, it will be a fault tomorrow also. And as one says, "for punishment

---

8. From the Latin legal maxim "veritatem dies aperit."

9. Seneca, *De Ira* 3.12.4, in vol. 1, *Moral Essays*, 285.

10. In the ancient world, the spleen was associated with the emotions of anger.

11. Plutarch, *On the Control of Anger*, 133.

postponed can still be exacted, but once exacted it cannot be recalled."[12] "Such power, though deferred, will not perish. Wait for the time when the order will be our own; at the moment we shall speak under the dictation of anger."[13]

Stop and Think about Your Anger

Fourth, let angry people stop and think about their anger and ask whether they intend to ever lay it aside. If the answer is yes, then would it not be better to leave their anger than for their anger to leave them? Wouldn't it be better for them to vanquish their anger than to be overcome by it? Wouldn't it be better to quench their anger with the water of the Spirit than for it to last until it burns out? Anger, like all other passions, will in time tire itself out, and angry people will fall down with their own ruin.

But on the other hand, if they purpose to never lay aside anger but to live in perpetual enmity against another, let them consider that they nourish in themselves a viper that will devour them from the inside out. For who is more vexed, grieved, and disturbed by anger than the person enslaved to this passion? And is there anything that sooner cuts off the thread of life than the sharpness of fretful grief?

---

12. Seneca, *De Ira* 2.22.4, in vol. 1, *Moral Essays*, 215.
13. Seneca, *De Ira* 3.31.2, in vol. 1, *Moral Essays*, 333.

Then let angry people consider how much good time they waste in a bad way. Time is so short and precious and should be better esteemed and employed. For example, we should use our time in seeking to make friends rather than lose them through unjust anger or in reconciling with enemies rather than exasperating them by wronging them in new ways. And we should use our time in performing Christian works of love and mercy so that we may hear that comforting sentence on the last day, "Come, ye blessed of my Father, inherit the kingdom prepared for you from the foundation of the world: for I was an hungered, and ye gave me meat," and so forth (Matt. 25:34–35) rather than in doing the works of the flesh, among which anger is numbered (Gal. 5:20), and for which those who commit them shall not inherit the kingdom of God but hear the fearful sentence, "Depart from me, ye cursed, into everlasting fire, prepared for the devil and his angels" (Matt. 25:41).

Pray for the Holy Spirit's Help

The last and primary means both for keeping us from falling into anger and for subduing anger after it has taken hold of us is sincere, heartfelt prayer to God, that He would grant us the gracious assistance of His Holy Spirit. For by the Spirit our affections may be so ruled and sanctified that they are freed from natural corruption and become useful for the glory of God, the good of our brothers, and the furthering of our own salvation.

It is only the water of the Spirit and the shield of faith that are able to quench the fury of our passions. And prayer is a primary means for obtaining these spiritual graces from the hands of God (Luke 11:13).

CHAPTER 12

Remedies to Cure Anger in Others

Having considered the remedies for curing anger in ourselves, we now come to the remedies by which we may cure anger in others.

Be Silent

The first way to respond to anger in another person is to use silence. For as fire cannot long continue without wood, so anger cannot long endure when words and cross answers are not multiplied.

On the other hand, cross words and stubborn replies make the angry person proceed from anger to rage, from folly to fury and madness. This is what the wise man teaches us: "As coals are to burning coals, and wood to fire; so is a contentious man to kindle strife" (Prov. 26:21). "The wringing of the nose bringeth forth blood: so the forcing of wrath bringeth forth strife" (Prov. 30:33).

By silence you may therefore more quickly abate another person's anger. But cross answers turn anger into violent rage. For as the cannon shot loses its force when it lands in soft earth or wool but dashes a wall of stone into pieces, so the violence of the most furious anger is abated when answered with silence but furiously rages on when met with opposition.

This is why Plato called anger the nerves of the mind, or "sinews of the soul," which are "intensified by harshness and relaxed by gentleness."[1] Therefore, if you would pacify another's wrath, follow the counsel of Jesus, the son of Sirach, who said, "Strive not with a man that is full of tongue, and heap not wood upon his fire" (Ecclesiasticus 8:3).[2] For, as he notes, as wood increases the fire, so multiplying words increases anger.

Answer Softly

But silence is not always expedient, especially when someone has a just and honest reason for anger. For often the angry person will think that silence communicates contempt, as though you were silent because you scornfully refused to even answer them. Therefore, the second remedy, a soft and mild answer, is sometimes a more suitable remedy for curing anger in others. By a soft answer you either excuse yourself by showing your innocence, or you humbly confess your wrong and seek forgiveness.

---

1. Quoted in Plutarch, *On Moral Virtue* 449, in vol. 6, *Plutarch's Moralia*, trans. W. C. Helmbold, Loeb Classical Library, no. 337 (Cambridge, Mass.: Harvard University Press, 1962), 71.

2. On Ecclesiasticus, see note 1 in chapter 8.

And this is the medicine the wise physician prescribes: "A soft answer turneth away wrath: but grievous words stir up anger" (Prov. 15:1). "By long forbearing is a prince persuaded, and a soft tongue breaketh the bone" (Prov. 25:15). Or, as it is in the original, "a man of bone"—that is, a person who is stiff and stubborn. We see an example of this in Abigail, who, by her mild and discreet words, quickly appeased David's furious anger (1 Sam. 25:24).

As a red-hot iron when dipped in cold water loses all its heat and returns to its natural coldness, so can the heat of the hottest anger be cooled with a soft answer. On the other hand, cross and ill-chosen words will cause the least spark of anger to flame out into fury. We see this in the example of Moses. Though he was the meekest man on earth (Num. 12:3), yet he was provoked to wrath by the contentious wrangling of the people. Thus, he grievously offended God through his rash words, as appears from comparing Numbers 20:10–11 with Psalm 106:32–33. If you blow on a spark, it will increase into a flame, but if you spit on it, the flame will be quenched—and both proceed from the mouth. In the same way, cross words will turn the least spark of anger into furious rage, but a soft answer will easily appease it.

Gently Admonish

Once other people's anger has passed, the last remedy is to gently admonish them, that they might learn the great evils that follow anger. It does no good to feed someone while they are nauseous, for they will just vomit the food up again. In the same way, it is pointless to attempt the cure of anger by giving advice until the angry fit has passed and its heat has been somewhat assuaged. For as long as people are ruled by their passions, they either will not or cannot listen to reason. When a man's house is on fire, he hears almost nothing because of the noise of the crowd, the crackling of the fire, and the alarm of his own mind. So it is with angry people: the violence of this affection and fury of this passion make people in a fit of rage deaf to all reason. Therefore, they are to be admonished after the fury has somewhat spent itself. Then the great evils of anger in respect to their souls and bodies, their neighbors and friends, the church and the nation can be presented to their more sober meditations.

But those who admonish others must remember to use all gentleness and discretion in their admonition. Otherwise, they will provoke further anger, even as they try to prevent it. For if they are too austere or too rough in using harsh words and bitter rebukes, they not only show an absurd contradiction by reproving anger with anger but also make their admonitions useless. For in seeing their sharpness and severity, angry people will not confess or labor to amend their fault but rather defend it by aggravating the injuries they have received. No one will allow their wound to be searched by a surgeon with rough hands and a hard heart, and no patients will commit themselves to the care of a merciless physician. In the same way, no one (much less an angry person) can endure to have their bitter faults rubbed in their face. Nor will the wounds and diseases of their minds be healed and cured with the overly sharp medicine of bitter, insolent words.

Therefore, those who reprove anger with anger are not fit physicians for those who are subject to this passion. For angry persons will cover their imperfections and say they are well rather than show their symptoms to a bad-tempered physician, or they will justify and defend their anger as lawful and necessary. A frightened snake, when it has no way to escape, will turn and attack the one who pursues it. When the timid stag can no longer escape by running, it will turn and make a stand, turning cowardly fear into desperate rage. In the same way, when an angry person being harshly pursued with sharp words and bitter rebukes has no cause or excuse to cover her fault or hope of pity if she confesses it, she will turn on the one who reproves her. She will point out the greater faults of her accuser in order to extenuate her own. "You have greater faults than mine," she will say; "therefore, you should cure yourself before you try to become another person's physician. Indeed, you are no more innocent than I am. If you were in the same circumstances, you would be angry too. You may seem sweet and harmless, but you are not without your bitter gall."

In a word, the angry man will never cry *peccavi* (I have sinned) unless afterward with some confidence he may add *miserere*[3] (have mercy); neither will he suffer his wounds to be cured by someone who, by their rough handling, will more vex him than please him by providing the cure.

---

3. A *miserere* is a psalm in which one seeks mercy, such as Psalm 51.

Conclusion

May all those who find themselves subject to this unruly passion of anger carefully apply to themselves the remedies and medicines we must use for the curing of anger, either in ourselves or in others. It will not benefit a sick man to merely read his physician's prescription or carry the medicine in his pocket. If he wants to get well, he must take the medicine according to the doctor's orders. Nor will this medicine for the soul be useful for the cure of anger unless you apply it to your heart and conscience.

But seeing that we are not able to even think a good thought on our own but that it is God alone who works in us both the will and the deed (2 Cor. 3:5; Phil. 2:13), let us seek the Lord, the only true physician. May He anoint the blind eyes of our understanding with the precious eye salve of His Holy Spirit, that we might see the deformities of this disordered affection, along with all others. And may He also by the same Spirit enable us to reform and renew our affections, that their violence and fury being abated and their filth and corruption being purged, cleansed, and sanctified, they may become useful for setting forth God's glory, the good of our brethren, and the furthering of our eternal salvation.

And this grace He has given to us through Him who died for us, Jesus Christ the righteous, to whom, along with the Father and the Holy Spirit, be honor, glory, power, and dominion, forever and ever. Amen.